THINKING AS A CHRISTIAN
ABOUT CHRISTIANITY

THINKING AS A CHRISTIAN ABOUT CHRISTIANITY

JOHN J. BRUGALETTA

RESOURCE *Publications* · Eugene, Oregon

THINKING AS A CHRISTIAN ABOUT CHRISTIANITY

Resource Publications
An Imprint of Wipf and Stock Publishers
199 W. 8th Ave., Suite 3
Eugene, OR 97401

www.wipfandstock.com

PAPERBACK ISBN: 978-1-6667-5740-8
HARDCOVER ISBN: 978-1-6667-5741-5
EBOOK ISBN:978-1-6667-5742-2

09/29/22

These essays were previously published in the venues indicated, sometimes in a slightly different form.
Agape Review, "Rousseau in the House of the Lord" and "*Agape* Love in the Bible"
CSL N.Y. C. S. Lewis Society, "C. S. Lewis and the Wait [sic} of Glory
Solum Literary Press, "The Concept of Evil" and "Forgiving as Process"

To Charles Dominick

CONTENTS

C.S. Lewis and the Wait [Sic] of Glory   1

Agape Love in the Bible   9

Forgiving as Process   12

The Concept of Evil   18

Rousseau in the House of the Lord   20

Real Presence and Remembrance   25

Judea as Death in the Gospel of John   31

"Something Understood" The Making of Christian Poetry in Our Time   33

An Introduction to Acted Parables in the Gospels   47

The Trinity   53

Are Some People Dogs?   57

"Remove This Cup from Me"   61

Jesus on the Family   63

The Nativity   68

Faithful Artist, Faithful Art   72

Bibliography   79

C.S. LEWIS AND THE WAIT [SIC] OF GLORY

IT'S NOT TERRIBLY HARD to wait in line briefly at a grocery check stand, or in a movie line, because in both cases two things are in our favor: we know what the result of waiting will be, and the wait is usually not terribly long. How much harder it is when the outcome is uncertain or the wait interminable, when, for example, a candidate for a job waits to hear the results of yesterday's interview; or the student waits for a grade on a difficult exam; or parents wait weeks, months, even years for news of a missing child.

And yet a certain kind of waiting, what might be called "dynamic waiting" or "active waiting" is a major commandment of the New Testament. Jesus himself uses two words in Greek for this kind of waiting, both a form of the word *gregoreo,* and both of which mean "be watchful," "be awake." Today we might phrase it, "Don't live your life on cruise control." "Keep watch," he says in Matt 24:42, "because you do not know on what day your Lord will come." "Keep watch," he says again in Mark 13:35, "because you do not know when the owner of the house will come back." "It will be good for those servants," he says in Luke 12:37, "whose master finds them watching when he comes." And we can't quibble over the limitations of language here. New Testament Greek had a word for a more passive kind of waiting; it is *prosedeketo,* and it is used in Luke 23:51 of Joseph of Arimathea.

But the most frightening use of these words for active waiting is in the gospel of Matthew when Christ has taken Peter, James and

John with him to Gethsemane to "watch"—that is, to keep awake, stay alert, pray—with him. They fail in this, and their failure seems to have consequences, terrible ones. (Luke 23:51)

I don't for a moment think their failure lay in their sleepiness, any more than it was the fault of that poor fig tree that it was fruitless in the off season. The incidents are acted parables, the one in Gethsemane expressing a commandment to be conscious of our lives and of our relationship with God.

But the most urgent and compelling use of the word is in Jesus' eschatological discourse in the gospel of Mark, the first line of which I've already quoted. Here it is in full:

> Therefore keep watch because you do not know when the owner of the house will come back—whether in the evening, or at midnight, or when the rooster crows, or at dawn. If he comes suddenly, do not let him find you sleeping. What I say to you, I say to everyone: "Watch!"

And here is the point I'd like to discuss. This active stillness, this dynamic tranquility, this "watching," is the wait of glory. It is not only a wait *for* the Son of Man who will come again in glory; it is also a wait in which our active pursuits while waiting make all the difference in the outcome, in which the thing waited for is profoundly involved in our mode of waiting, and so a wait *of* glory. In the parable, whether the servant is feeding or beating his fellow servants when the master returns makes all the difference in the master's treatment of him; the five bridesmaids who brought oil for their lamps get into the wedding hall, while the five who neglected to do this are locked out; in the parable of the talents, the servants who kept their gifts active and productive were rewarded with greater gifts, while the servant who kept his gift inactive and unproductive is given only weeping and gnashing of teeth. (Matt 24,25)

Do you see where we are? There are now no artificial divisions between the student's studying, being tested, and waiting for the results; no divisions between the job-seeker's schooling, interview, and waiting for the decision. It is all one. It is this life. As Lewis says in "The World's Last Night":

> Taken by themselves, these considerations [of the pos-
> sible immediacy of the Apocalypse] might seem to invite
> a relaxation of our efforts for the good of posterity: but if
> we remember that what may be upon us at any moment
> is not merely an End but a Judgment, they should have
> no such result.[1]

We cannot relax our efforts because our efforts are part and parcel of our judgment and potential glory. However, he goes on to say, "Neither should we indulge in 'frantic panaceas,' sacrificing the lives and liberty of our contemporaries for the sake of a posterity that may never exist." As usual, Lewis strikes just the right note of temperance here, the sane middle ground between the extremes of apathy on the one hand and obsessive utopianism on the other.

But while it is an important first step to say "Avoid extremes," it is not enough. Merely saying it tends to leave a pale and ineffectual middle way in the imaginations of most people. "Compromise" is a word often used to condemn it. Now I am not opposed to compromise when antagonists cannot agree on all their demands. But there is something better than compromise by a factor of ten, and it is called synthesis. Compromise is weaker than either extreme; synthesis is stronger than its extremes. We tend to think in the modern world that only extremes are strong, so we tend to be blind to this far greater—though quieter—power of synthesis.

Consider the conflicting urges humanity has always felt with regard to sex. There is the urge to unrestricted frequency and unlimited partners. We don't all of us feel it all of the time, but most of us feel it some of the time. That is one extreme. The other is just as natural a human urge, the hunger for celibacy, and it is not always the hangover effect of debauchery. Now some societies accommodate the first extreme with institutionalized prostitution, certain puberty rites and other social devices, while others accommodate the opposite extreme, as the Essenes apparently did, and certain gnostic sects. But the synthesis of these opposites is not merely moderation; it is a third thing: marriage.

---

1. Lewis, *World's Last Night*, 111.

Monogamous marriage does not offer an average number of sex partners between 1 and 500. Nor does it prescribe a frequency of sexual contact midway between 1 and 5,000. A healthy monogamous marriage might contain even more than 5,000 acts of love, or it may need no more than a few. It is not a mathematical computation; it is a stroke of genius.

Marriage was known long before the Christian era began, but the church accepted it, taking Christ's first miracle as a sign of approval even more authoritative than St. Paul's grudging permission. But in another unexpected stroke, the church also allows one (but not both) of the extremes: celibacy. And then there is alcohol. As Lewis has pointed out, Christianity is not the prohibitionist religion; Islam is that. But while a certain surprising synthesis, called communion, is the stroke of genius at the center, teetotalers also are allowed. I personally think this is another instance of God's mercy towards us; I suspect He'd rather we took communion in both species, but if it makes us ill He won't insist. But He seems to abhor drunkenness. It could also be argued, and plausibly I think, that Christian Trinitarianism is the right synthesis of a loose polytheism and an overly rigid monotheism.

Before Lewis led me back to God, I suffered intolerable fits of worrying over the state of the world. I fretted over injustices petty and large, over the state of the environment, over world politics, over nearly everything. It was as if every problem was my problem and every burden my burden. One of my pleasures on becoming a Christian was the relief I felt on learning there was Someone in charge, Someone trustworthy, and His name was Yahweh. That was faith. A little later I learned I still had duties, but I was only one member of a world-wide body of people who were trying to take part in God's work. It was St. Paul's metaphor of the church as a body with differing members, organs if you like—hands, heads, feet, chests, backs for burdens. That is God's synthesis with regard to duties. No one person, no one family, can support even a relatively small local church financially, but if we each do our best, we won't need to fret over our church's budget. And "doing our best" is our next look at the wait of glory.

Nothing was so useful in my learning to actively wait as the ending of Lewis's essay on "The Inner Ring," where he counsels young people to make their work their focus, to become sound craftsmen. Among other things, work makes the wait more bearable. In talking with a famous Christian author and psychoanalyst once, I suddenly realized how well simple work can function as a natural tranquilizer. He said his teenage son had gone with friends to spend the evening in a neighborhood known for its dangers. The boy had promised to come home by a certain hour. You know the story. My friend waited, tried to keep calm, paced, called hospitals, police, paced some more. Finally, to tame his frantic mind, he went down to his basement and started cleaning it. There he was, cleaning and waiting at 4 a.m. when the son arrived.

And when will the Son of God arrive? That is what we are waiting for, isn't it? And a long wait we've had of it too, over 2,000 years, when we originally believed the return would be almost immediate. We Christians have become pre-eminent among the world's adepts at waiting. If anyone can tell you how to wait without knowing either the exact outcome or how long this wait will last, or even whether it will end in his lifetime, a good Christian can. He or she will probably quote you something like Paul's letter to Titus:

> Our people must learn to devote themselves to doing what is good [kalon ergon=good works], in order that they may provide for daily necessities and not live unproductive lives. (3:14)

Or his second letter to the Thessalonians:

> We hear that some among you are idle. They are not busy; they are busybodies. Such people we command and urge in the Lord Jesus Christ to settle down and earn the bread they eat. (3:11–12)

But when I read the words "provide for daily necessities" and "earn the bread they eat," I think of Lewis's essay "Good Work and Good Works." Things were bad in Lewis's day, but they seem even worse in our own time; it is less likely every day that the young will find jobs that pay a living wage for work that would be worthwhile even without the money it brings. Watch a good stonemason lay a hearth and chimney and your heart sings for the gracefulness of those hands, the eloquent economy of those motions. Watch a glassblower make a bottle, a cobbler stitch a shoe. Watch a baker kneading dough or a stone carver coaxing flowers and faces out of the dead stone, and that will raise your standards too high to appreciate the movements of most ballet dancers.

In fact, watch anybody do anything with a heartfelt sense that it is honest work, work that serves God and one's fellows, and you will see the joy in that work translated into a mime of prayer. Zen Buddhism takes it to an extreme in the tea ceremony, with the perfunctory act of replacing the water ladle formalized into the ringing of the water pot like a bell. Brother Lawrence (a 17th century Carmelite friar) was more to the point for us. We are told that he was never hasty nor loitering, but did each thing in its season, with an even, uninterrupted composure and tranquility of spirit. "The time of business," said he, "does not with me differ from the time of prayer, and in the noise and clatter of my kitchen, while several persons are at the same time calling for different things, I possess God in as great tranquility as if I were on my knees at the blessed sacrament."[2]

Here is yet another way in which to envision the truth in what Lewis says when he tells us faith and works are like the two blades of a scissors. You can't separate them and expect them to work; you can't have just one of them and expect to cut things easily with that. And here we have them, fused inextricably and common as the grass. We are all of us, or can be, as consecrated as bishops, and when we lay hands on a task we can bless it. Here is the stroke of genius at the center, both uniting and avoiding the extreme temptations to be idle and to be a busybody.

But if we do our jobs in a different spirit, only for the money in them, or the sense of prestige or power we derive from them, they become no more than an inflating of our egos. We then "sell" our moment of present time for some promised reward later. The work of Christian waiting is not a "deal"; it is our gift back to God.

2. Brother Lawrence, *Practice of the Presence of God*, 20.

If it were a deal, its poverty of size and its derivative nature would make it ludicrously inadequate. As it is, however, the person who prepares a good meat loaf to feed four, and the missionary who converts thousands are both only adding small nudges to great hills of prior acts, though both nudges are also felt in some way throughout the cosmos. I can imagine angels cheering at a well-planted tree or a well-swept floor.

But it's hard for me to imagine angels cheering for the act of prostitution. For the prostitute or the trick when they stop sinning, yes—uproarious cheering, whistling and clapping of wings and stamping of feet (on clouds, I suppose). But not for the sin. If good work is a benediction, shoddy work is prostitution of our talents and a sin.

We live in a world of prostitutes and in a world of tricks. I have watched our young people year after year take majors at the university that promise (they think) six-figure salaries, majors that they detest, or at the very least will bore them. They are like the man who marries for money, though he loathes the woman's conversation and finds her personality disgusting. He will pay for the money that comes with her, and his payment will be measured out in miserable days, the same miserable days suffered by the grudging worker who does only what is necessary, fills a space, calculates what he will get out of it, is disappointed no matter what the outcome, and hates his life.

There are so many reasons for shoddy workmanship, and they are so embedded in society, that it is nearly impossible for most of us to avoid committing this sin. How many of us, to use Lewis's phrase once more, can do for a living what we would do anyway if we were independently wealthy? Or in Robert Frost's words, how many of us can unite our vocations with our avocations, make our jobs and hobbies the same? Not many, obviously. But once again Lewis seems to have the only realistic answer: that we must remain aware of the problem while we are caught in it, not allowing ourselves to accept present conditions as normal; we must "watch," not merely wait. And when we are offered the chance to do something honest and wholesome for a living we must leap at it. And we must give more in our work than we are paid for.

7

It's not an easy thing to be a Christian. Those who scorn Christianity as a way of sugar-coating this tragic life have no idea how pitifully ignorant they sound. There is no harder way to live than to be constantly at the point of tension between extremist seductions. We are always trying to find the synthesis, the sweet spot, between the extremes of environmentalism and the extremes of human use of the earth, between extremist feminism and extremist masculinism, between an extremist scorn for the flesh as "a sack of dung" and an extremist idolatry of the flesh as glorious in and of itself. It is a burden we carry, a burden that would be intolerable were it not made light for us by the faith inherent in the act of dynamic waiting for glory.

When seeking the point of active stillness between this world and the coming one, it can be helpful to think of this world as a play by a great Author, as Lewis does. Remember his metaphor? We don't know whether we're in Act I or Act V. We don't know who are the major characters and who the minor ones. We can't guess the plot because we are in the play; we can't see it in its entirety as the Author does. We are often tempted, as actors are, either to forget that our lives offstage are more real than our dramatic roles; or, to take the opposite tack, we're tempted to yearn so strongly for the real, to grow so disillusioned with our assigned roles that we scheme to exit early, ruining a part of the play.

For although the play is not true reality, it matters nevertheless. Evidently it matters immensely. Like all great drama, it is not mere entertainment. It means something, and we mean something within it, so long as we do an honest, craftsmanlike job with our roles. For those who neither sit impassive while waiting for the curtain, nor argue that the plot should be rewritten, but who remember always that their most trivial-seeming word may be the "last syllable of recorded time," there is glory in the green room

AGAPE LOVE IN THE BIBLE

IN THE NEW TESTAMENT, the Greek term *agape* occurs over 200 times, and all Bible scholars translate the term as "love." But while *agape* has only one meaning, the English word "love," when used as a noun, has thirteen meanings. It can mean affection, enthusiasm, a score of zero in tennis, or to do something freely (as opposed to "for money") and more. And there are six similar meanings when the word is used as a verb.

The result of this disorder for the Bible translator is the Christian public's erroneous assumption that Scripture commands us to at least have kind feelings for everyone else, and at worst to have erotic emotions for them.

But there are today, as there always have been, people for whom *honest* Christians cannot produce even kind feelings. Who among us can do so when faced with a Hitler, or Vlad the Impaler, or Ivan the Terrible? And for those who are not familiar with these three examples, let's imagine a madman who had a habit of kidnapping women and burying them alive. Loving him, in the popular sense, would mean disobeying what is in Holy Scripture. As an example of Jesus' low evaluation of certain people, "Woe to you, scribes and Pharisees, hypocrites, because you travel about on sea and land to make one proselyte; and when he becomes one, you make him twice as much a son of hell as yourselves." (Matt 23:15)

But the good news is that *agape* love does not necessarily include feelings as a prompt. It is simply an ingrained habit of doing what, to the best of our knowledge, would be best for someone else. It is our way of following what God does in answering our prayers:

if He considers our petitionary prayer to be helpful, He will send us that for which we prayed. If not, He will send nothing. He does this, I believe, to protect us from ourselves. It is also something He seems to have implanted in us, for when our toddler demands an authentic pistol, something like instinct tells us to refuse, despite the young one's shrieks of protest.

(And here it must be said that often in our lives there are other kinds of love that can combine with *agape* love. For example *philia* or friendship love may sit beside it when actual friends are considered; and *eros* or romantic love might be present as well. But while these differing types of love may at times be correlated, they are special cases, for *agape* love remains as itself no matter what is added.)

A search through various Bible versions reveals that *agape* is routinely translated as "love," so of course the majority of pastors and priests use this misleading word in their sermons. These versions include 1890 Darby Bible, American Standard Version, Christian Standard Bible, English Standard Version, Four Gospels, God's Word Translation, Good News Bible, Good News for Modern Man, Holman Christian Standard Version, International Standard Version, Jerusalem Bible, King James Version, Lexham English Bible, The Message, Net Bible, New American Standard Bible: 1995, New Century Version, New English Bible, New International Version, New Living Bible, New Revised Standard Version, New World Translation, Restoration Bible, The Story of Redemption Bible, and The World English Bible.

This list demonstrates the unseen cause of Christians' confusion when faced with putting God's will to use in their lives. There are two words in the English language that would more accurately translate *agape,* "concern (or concerned)" and "benevolent (or benevolence)." The passage in the Gospel of Matthew which now reads, "love your neighbor as yourself," could be translated as, "be as *concerned* for your neighbor as you are for yourself," or "be as *benevolent* toward your neighbor as you are for yourself." (Matt 19:19b) It must be added that there are approximately 26 passages in three of the gospels—Mark does not use the term— that make this mistake. They are as follows: Matt 5:43, 5:44, 6:24,

19:19, 22:37, 24:12; Luke 6:32, 6:35, 7:42, 11:42, 11:11:43; John 5:42, 10:17, 13:34 (3 times), 14:15, 14:23, 14:31, 15:9, 15:10, 15:13, 15:17, 17:26, 21:15, 21:16.

So what is to be done about this aberration? It has taken root so widely among Christian denominations that it will take strenuous efforts by a large number of people to set it right. Let's pray that this becomes a reality.

FORGIVING AS PROCESS

EVERY FEW MONTHS THE news includes a case in which someone has been grievously and maliciously injured or offended. The law has been broken, the police have arrested the offender, and the system of law is about to punish the defendant, when the victim (or the victim's survivor) forgives him and refuses to file charges. Sometimes the offender is so shocked by this that he repents and changes his ways. But this is not always the outcome; often enough, the offender, now free again, goes on to injure someone else, perhaps many others.

Christians who believe that forgiveness must always include immediate and unconditional restoration of the offender to a status of complete trust have various ways of dealing with the fact that unrepentant offenders exist. They will ignore them, or deny that they exist, or trust in the fact that some offenders repent and assume there is some process invisibly at work to heal the others. It may be so eventually, but if so, it often happens after death, in a state of being that we are not told about.

The premise of this essay is that Christian forgiveness is a two-part process. And this is especially clear when we consider that the people affected by our decision to trust automatically are not only the offender and ourselves, but any number of other people in the future. The murderer who goes unpunished and who murders again is not the only person guilty of his crime and his sin; so is his rash forgiver. And while we most likely will not know those people who will be his victims, they too are children of God and are worthy of our care. The fact that most of us will treat them as non-existent because we cannot easily imagine what they look like does not excuse our act of putting their lives in danger.

The burglar who has stolen that jewelry left to us by a beloved grandparent; the co-worker who "keyed" our new car, ripping through the paint; the fellow church member who slyly undercuts our reputation by innuendo; the trusted spouse who deceived us; the baby-sitter who molested our child—each of these offenders injects a dose of acid into our hearts, leaving an internal wound that can fester for a lifetime if left alone.

Judaism releases this once each year, commanding forgiveness every Rosh Hashanah. Christianity expands this one day to every day of every year of our lives. "Forgive us our trespasses," we repeat, "as we forgive those who trespass against us" (Matt 6:12). Without our learning how to forgive others, we will not be forgiven. To anyone who believes in a just and holy God, this poses a horrifying prospect.

So just exactly *how are we* to forgive others? Christians often quote that astonishing prayer Jesus prayed from the cross on behalf of His assassins: "Forgive them, Father, for they know not what they do" (Luke 23:34). But in fact we are so astonished by the prodigious forgiveness of it that we do not listen to it carefully. "For they know not what they do" presupposes that if they *did* know what they were doing, the offense would not be so readily forgivable. Clearly there are conditions presumed when forgiving "those who trespass against us."

The question, surely, is not whether presumed conditions exist, but rather what these conditions might be. For this we must look to the internal workings of offense, both in the offended and in the offender. The offended person's experience is one of having been violated; one's sense of security or of trust in another person has suffered a rupture. The violation ordinarily would give rise either to a desire for revenge (an outward action expressing anger) or to depression (a turning inward of one's anger). The former is a pre-Christian or non-Christian norm; the latter is often mistaken for the Christian norm.

This sense of having been violated, with its attendant anger, can act on the offended Christian like an injected acid, eating its way through the spirit. Retaining this acidic reaction can lead only to continued self-injury, and possibly to an act of vengeance beyond the control of wisdom.

The first task then, after suffering an offense, is to rid oneself of the sense of injury. Surprisingly, doing this first requires that the offended party abandon the perverse pleasure of holding a grudge. Once the violation is no longer seen as a financial transaction—one in which injury is exchanged for injury—it begins to be possible to look for the offender's motivations and point-of-view. This is not as easy or as immediate as some think it is. At times, and for some people, praying for the renewal of the offender's personality can help the offended who is praying. Another technique that I have recently heard about is to "bind" the offense to the past, not "loosing" it to create havoc in the present. But no matter how offenses are treated, those who do not see the complexity of forgiveness believe it to be a matter of an instant's decision.

It can of course be almost that simple if the injury was unintentional. The driver who accidentally ran over our dog or our spouse might see a temporary spate of anger in us, but, assuming there was no reckless driving involved, we know this person is not culpable. But when sincere and genuine, most acts of forgiveness are a process, moving from the removal of resentment to the final restoration of the former relationship. True, forgiveness requires a decision at the outset, but like the decision to rebuild a bombed place of prayer, much work must follow the decision. And if one is just beginning to learn the process of forgiveness, the learning curve can be either long or steep.

One vital lesson to be learned by the new forgiver is that even complete removal of the sense of injury does not completely take one back to the relationship the offended had with the offender before the violation. To heal the injury in the offended person solves only that person's internal problem. There is no assurance that it solves the offender's problem, which may be the habit or tendency of offending, violating or harming again, perhaps toward others. This lack of assurance not only can be, it often is the case even when the offended party's attitude toward the offender has become once again sincerely characterized by *agape* love. Love can solve many problems in relationships, but only when it has been truly adopted (or become adoptable) into the lives of *both* parties. Love from the victim can change the offender's life only if the offender is currently seeking a loving *agape* relationship, whether consciously or unconsciously. Perhaps that is why Jesus tells his disciples, "If [your brother] repents, forgive him" (Luke 17:3). The word "repents" here translates the Greek word *metanoese,* which means a change of mind, a turning away. This is more than saying, "I'm sorry," and more than a feeling of remorse. It is a sharp turn in the direction of one's life.

Christian love, when felt by the offended for the offender, carries with it the temptation to immediately replace one's trust in the offender. But do we trust even an obedient toddler to safely handle explosives? Do we trust a normal chimpanzee with our crystal collection? Do we indulge our love of nature by setting free our flatulent St. Bernard dog in our house when it is filled with asthmatic guests? These examples of misplaced trust may well seem laughable because they are so unlikely, but as hypothetical examples, they accurately characterize how we can have benevolent thoughts toward someone without necessarily trusting them in certain circumstances. We may love the toddler and have great affection for the exotic pets, but to trust them utterly would be to endanger not only others but themselves as well.

It is true that the act of trusting even such inappropriate caretakers can occasionally help an adolescent or immature adult in gaining self-esteem, but only if their maturation has reached the point at which they display signs of being trustworthy. The question then is how we might determine whether or not an offender, one who has shown dangerous tendencies in the past, has become trustworthy in the present. Is an apology enough for renewed and total trust? Would this be enough, coming as it might from a babysitter who molested your child, for you once again to entrust your child to this person? If so, perhaps you are more concerned with your own sanctity, as characterized by your own ability to forgive, than you are with the safety of your child. There are usually more than one or two people involved in an injury, and if we disregard the safety of any one of them we are committing an injustice and, one would think, a sin.

Let's imagine that a man has killed your son. The murderer has been arrested, and the police ask you to bring charges against him. He confesses his crime and says he repents. (This is a scenario that will sound familiar to anyone who reads a newspaper regularly.) Will you forgive him? If you are a Christian, of course you will. Will you bring a charge of homicide against him? I will argue that you are bound to do so. But why would you do so despite your having forgiven him? Because, while you no longer hate him, you are in no position to trust him. If he is released because of you and kills again, you will be an accessory to his later murders. You have in fact, if not legally then morally, aided and abetted his murdering others. You carry some of his guilt because you refused to help the authorities in keeping the public safe from such dangerous people.

The first stage in forgiveness, the part we are to enact "seventy times seven" times, is to no longer hold a grudge against those who "trespass against us." But we do not refuse to rehire the child-molesting babysitter because of a grudge; we refuse to rehire her because (a) we do not want to expose our child (whom we also love) to injury, and (b) we do not want the child-molester to molest more children, implying approval of her illness and adding to her guilt.

And this principle of restraining love is perhaps why God does not yet forgive the unrepentant sinner. "Forgive us our trespasses as we forgive those who trespass against us" is expressed in the form of rabbinic rhetoric. The meaning behind it is true, but that truth has been cast into parallelism. The reason we cannot both expect God's forgiveness and then refuse to forgive others is evident when we think of the servant in the parable who was forgiven much but would not forgive his debtor. His request on his own behalf was evidently not a plea from a state of humility; it was hypocritical, a scam used against a compassionate master.

When applied to the entire panoply of human acts of forgiveness, a similar hypocrisy appears in those who expect God to forgive their sins and then, when confronted with sins against themselves by a neighbor, conveniently forget that they themselves are sinners. The saying "There, but for the grace of God, go I" has never occurred to them. In addition to being hypocrites, they are guilty of overweening pride. Is it any wonder that God refuses to forgive their sins? They have not actually repented of those sins. How can they repent if they so quickly are able by implication to deny their own sinfulness? And if they are not repentant, turned from the direction of their sin, forgiving them would be the act of an enabler. God does not necessarily refuse to forgive the unrepentant sinner because He is angry with the sinner; he refuses to forgive the sinner because He loves him or her and does not want that soul to die in sin.

Forgiveness, it turns out, is not a simple matter. It is not something that emotions alone, or intellect alone, can wisely guide. Love and caution must go hand-in-hand in learning how to forgive. And we all must learn more than merely *to* forgive; we must learn *how* to forgive.

THE CONCEPT OF EVIL

THERE IS A WEB site that is open to questions of any variety, and then allows almost anyone to answer the question. Such was the case with the question, "What is the strongest argument against the existence of God?" The person who chose to reply said only, "The fact that there is evil in the world," implying by the brevity of his or her answer that the case was now closed (as it is for some philosophers). It interests me that a person who believes there is no God should choose the word "evil," for the word is meaningful only when uttered by someone who does not confuse sorrows with the utter absence of good.

And this confusion is not only difficult to avoid by the human race, it is almost impossible. Even Voltaire, that brilliant man, was shocked (though probably not personally inconvenienced) that a benevolent God should allow the widely destructive 1755 earthquake in Lisbon, Portugal. Again and again, when war costs many lives, or infants die, or pandemics threaten the survival of millions, the word evil is either applied or implied.

My point here is not that these should be passed over like missing a meal; it is that we, with our limited knowledge and wisdom, are not competent to apply the word evil to anything in our experience, especially when a cosmic force is implied.

Consider the following illustration. A toddler watches while her father buries her dead guinea pig in the family rose bed. The father, sensing the child's grief, tells her that the animal will turn into a rose one day (as it would, in a sense). But the toddler, having no knowledge of plant growth, says, "You're not telling me the truth."

Because her extreme youth gave her no way to understand her father's statement, she assumed that his attempt at consolation was a lie. And this case is parallel with that of many adults who speak of evil while having only a limited grasp of this complex problem.

Did we know, for example, that those who have made a study of the concept of evil have found it necessary to divide the examples into two types, a broad concept and a narrow concept? And then, with evil in the broad sense, there are again two types, natural evil and moral evil. And this is only an offhand look at a widespread field of study.

But even a superficial knowledge of religions will allow one to see that, among the three main faiths (Judaism, Christianity and Islam), only Christianity faces this problem called theodicy. It is only in Christianity that Christ's behavior and words are taken as true guides to the nature of God, and his nature turns out to be omniscient, omnipotent and benevolent. It is because of human interpretations of these three superlative and unimaginable traits that many afflicted people think there is no God at all. It seems to never occur to them that if God is omniscient, we creatures with inferior minds may never understand what happens in that extravagant and incomparable mind.

And so for the person who believes God does not exist, and who does so on the shaky platform of the existence of evil, there remains the existence of scientifically gathered evidence of a mind that existed at, or before, the Big Bang to explain. Scientists in multiple specialties have found that at the beginning of time and space there were at least fifteen "fine tunings," from the strength of gravity to the speed of light. Without these, cosmologists tell us, there would be no galaxies, and therefore no life in the universe. And if the powerful and highly intelligent mind existed when there was no space/time, we are faced with the problem of explaining what sort of Mind (and I now capitalize with certainty) this was.

ROUSSEAU IN THE
HOUSE OF THE LORD

ON OCTOBER 24, 1776, on a narrow street in the French village of Menilmontant, a man was knocked down by a large dog. That's it. It doesn't sound like enough of an incident to make the pages of a daily newspaper, but in fact it was the match that touched off an explosion that is still shaking the world today. The man was Jean-Jacques Rousseau, and the explosion is called Romanticism.

Rousseau later wrote that the "unforeseen accident," which had knocked him unconscious, "came to break the thread of [his] ideas and to give them for some time another direction."[1] And what was this direction? It turned out to be a fervent belief in the supreme value of the *self*, together with the vital importance of *isolation from civilization* and a permanent immersion in *nature*.

"And what," you ask, "is so wrong with that? Each of us *is* important to God. And cities *are* the locations of most crime greed and other forms of immorality. And nature *is* both beautiful and peaceful." And what you say is well said, but notice that you have left out some important words. Rousseau did not say the self was of value to God; he said it was of *supreme* value. When he describes the state of mind in which the accident put him, he calls it "a sufficing happiness, perfect and full. . .. So long as this state lasts, one suffices to oneself, like God."[2] Clearly such a person, in such a state, feels no need for the God of Christianity; he himself is god enough.

1. Rousseau, *Les Reveries Du Promeneur Solitaire*, Second Promenade.
2. Rousseau, *Les Reveries Du Promeneur Solitaire*, Fifth Promenade.

And a second vital word you have left out when speaking of the glories of nature is the word "permanent." Rousseau did not feel that a few days or weeks in the mountains were nearly enough. He didn't want a vacation. He wanted to live every day, and for the rest of his life, away from towns and alone. Now Jesus occasionally isolates himself, as in Mark 14:13, after He has heard of John the Baptist's death: "He withdrew from there in a boat, to a lonely place by himself." But the Lord never shows any interest in avoiding people permanently. He has too much concern for people to abandon them forever. Rousseau, on the other hand, doesn't really like people very much. He isn't Christ; he only feels he is. And for a Romantic, feeling is everything.

There is a phenomenon called the *zeitgeist,* the spirit of an age. Every age has one. The Christian Middle Ages lasted about 500 years, the Renaissance about 200, the Age of Reason 100. And every age has a different spirit, a different style, a different set of assumptions that it accepts automatically, without question, as an act of faith.

C. S. Lewis caught hold of one of these and shook it to death in his essay called, "We Have No Right to Happiness." Once he had said it, of course, we saw it made perfect sense. Of course it is insanity to believe that abandoning our spouse and children, just because another person makes us happy, is just and right. Thinking Jesus would approve of this is madness after reading Mathew 19:9, "I say to you, whoever divorces his wife, except for immorality, and marries another woman commits adultery." Jesus also encourages his followers to imitate his actions, as when after washing their feet, He says, "I have given you an example, so that you should do as I have done to you."

The question is, how are we to break its spell? How are we to see what the essential human life is like beyond the provincial confines of our temporal culture? Let's not make the mistake of thinking it would be to acquire an education, one that shows us how to try on for size the minds and hearts of people who lived at other times. For this will not help, because it doesn't tell us how to choose. We often end by blindly attempting to live like Joan of Arc, or Alexander the Great, or Wyatt Earp. No, the solution is not to *know* history, it is to *get out* of history. The answer is to see what human life looks like from outside of time, and as Christians we have the answer in our pockets. Our body of believers has lived through over 2000 years, much longer than any one age.

But in the early 19th century, Romantics like Samuel Taylor Coleridge found Christianity too dull to believe. The latest trend in thought was a new and exciting intoxication from nature. So we have poems like Coleridge's "The Eolian Harp" (a set of musical strings set in a window).[3] The poet addresses the poem to his Christian wife Sara, writing of the sounds as "sweet upbraiding," and "such a soft floating witchery of sound / As twilight elfins make."

But soon the poem takes a momentous step from appreciation of the wild beauties of nature to the realm of theological speculation. He writes:

> And what if all of animated nature
> Be but organic Harps diversely fram'd,
> That tremble into thought, as o'er them sweeps
> Plastic and vast, one intellectual breeze,
> At once the Soul of each, and God of all?

That is to say, what if every living being—including humans—were just dead eolian harps like the one in the window, and we come to life only when nature (the breeze) brought us temporarily to awareness (life) by making some sort of contact with us? If that is so, then isn't nature God? And isn't nature also our souls?

It is never safe playing with speculative theology; nevertheless, we see that Sara did not approve when he continues, "But thy more serious eye a mild reproof / Darts." He goes on in this poem to wish he may never without guilt speak of God except when he praises the Lord in awe "and with faith that *inly feels.*" This above all is what the Romantics wanted, something they could *feel,* something that *excited* them, some religion that made them feel young and in tune with nature again.

We have their descendants among us today, those extreme Romantics who tell us, as if they had a new revelation from heaven, that the stone-age peoples who believed every rock, every tree,

3. Magnuson, *Studies in Romanticism.*

every river and every mountain had its god or goddess were correct. Now I, for one, am ready to believe that we are stewards of the earth (Gen 1:28); and a good steward does not wantonly destroy the Master's property. But neither is the good steward a *worshipper* of the Master's property. He is a worshipper of the Master and respects the property as the Master's servant.

There are those Romantics among us who would, if they were in complete control of the world, return it to its state of nature before there were towns, agriculture or tame animals. But the good steward is not expected to practice cryogenics on the world, freezing it as if it were lent to us. As in Jesus' parable of the talents, the world was given us to be carefully used. We are in this world like guests in the home of a wealthy and generous person. When we are invited to sit at the table, should we refuse to eat the food offered? The owner of the house invited us; we are not thieves who broke in. Likewise, God put us here. Refusing to believe we have a rightful place in the ecosystem of the earth, as so many politically ultra-left people do today, strikes me as just plain rudeness toward our host, the Creator.

On the other hand, we are not to assume we are invulnerable within nature either. I think of the man who had grown up in this belief in the utter benevolence of nature, encouraged by Disney's "Bambi" and other cultural artifacts to see wild animals as other people wearing fur. He went to Africa to photograph lions, drove a van to a resting pride, left the window-mounted movie camera running as he walked up to the male and petted it. They never found a trace of the man, not even a shred of his clothing. They sent his camera to his widow in the United States. She had the film developed, then watched in horror as the lions enjoyed a new treat: breakfast in bed. He too evidently believed the Romantic lie, that "Nature never did betray the heart that loved her."[4]

Now the Lord is not an extreme anti-Romantic, for in Deuteronomy 25:4 He commands that an ox is not to be muzzled while it is threshing, that it should be allowed to feed on the grain below it. It is fairly definite that an accurate view of human life, lived as it

4. Wordsworth, *Borderers*.

was designed to be lived and ignoring all *zeitgeists*, is somewhere between extremes. It is neither gushingly sensitive nor callously cruel. It loves the self, but no more and no differently than it loves its neighbor. It seeks solitude on occasion, but it does not abandon society forever. It perceives faults in every aspect of the world—even in the church—but it perceives beauties and strengths as well.

"It's natural" is the contemporary way of saying a food or drug is safe. But nicotine is natural, as is rattlesnake venom. We also say it's natural about certain human tendencies, meaning often that they are acceptable. Some of my students, for example, even the Christians among them, believed romantic love is, and should be, more compelling in their lives than their religious beliefs. Romantic love is, in a word, more "natural" than religion. What happened to the Christian belief that the merely natural person is not qualified for salvation, that salvation requires a second birth which takes us beyond the natural?

I believe extreme Romanticism is a virus in our society today that is certainly harmful and maybe even deadly. Who can uproot it? The worldwide church perhaps, but I doubt it would have much of an effect because many denominations will fear a drop in the number of their members. The *via media* is not easy to impart, but I believe there are wonderful Christians today who can do it if they set their minds to it. Why shouldn't we try?

REAL PRESENCE AND
REMEMBRANCE

I WAS ONCE SEATED in a church about fifteen minutes early, when a man walked in and sat down beside me. Immediately he interrupted my prayers with the question, "Does this church still believe that Christ is really in the wafer and wine?" When I told him it did, he got up saying, "Well it should be understandable that it's all done in *memory* of Christ.," and he left that church, never to be seen there again.

I could cite some others who felt it was as important as belief in the Creeds to believe in the Eucharist as a device for Remembrance, rather than as the Real Presence of Jesus' body and blood or vice-versa. One of these instances caused a married couple to attend corporate worship at different denominations. It was encounters like these that led me to look into the background of the doctrine, the history, and the published debates.

Clearly one of the divisive topics in church-wide Christian doctrine is that of Presence in the Eucharist as opposed to Remembrance. In fairness to both positions, both may be said to be based on Scripture. In the synoptic gospels, Jesus does say they are his body and blood, and in Luke's gospel he immediately follows the breaking of bread by saying, "Do this in remembrance of me." Apparently some of the Real-Presence denominations give more weight to the first statements in each case, while those who see communion as remembrance favor the second. But Jesus said them both, so how is one to come to an accommodation of both passages?

As one who is admittedly trained in literary explication instead of biblical exegesis, I nevertheless propose to demonstrate that *both* may be seen as true, if only the synoptic gospels are considered together with the gospel of John. This I believe can be the solution to the division if it can be shown that when John, in 13: 26–27, indicates that Jesus dips a piece of bread, most probably in wine, for Judas Iscariot, the act constitutes communion, with either beneficial or dire consequences. The evangelist then comments, "After Judas took the piece of bread, Satan entered into him." (This sentence is read by some scholars as a way of timing the act rather than indicating cause and effect. But why would the evangelist try to indicate the timing?)

Was Satan's action a result of Judas' inappropriate communion? Did he fail in some way to "remember" Jesus while receiving the morsel? Some Bible scholars of the past seem to have thought so, but Adam Clarke's *Commentary* denies this, saying "Some have thought this morsel was the sacrament of the Lord's Supper, but this is an utter mistake." He then passes on to the next topic without stating his reasoning for thinking this a mistake.

But Clarke is merely more self-confident in this opinion than Raymond E. Brown is: "*Psomion* [morsel of food] has been used in Greek Christianity for the Eucharistic host, and so some scholars suggest that Jesus was giving the Eucharist to Judas. Loisy and W. Bauer use 1 Corinthians xi: 29, which speaks of the condemnation of those who eat the body of the Lord without discerning, to explain why Satan entered Judas after he ate the [Eucharistic] morsel. But would the writer [John] expect his readers to understand that the morsel was the Eucharist when he has not described the institution?"

Yet among the Church fathers, St. Ephraim, in his *Homilies*, paraphrases Jesus as saying "'As you have seen Me do, do also in My memory. Whenever you are gathered together in My name in Churches everywhere, do what I have done in memory of Me'" (4:6).[1] And St. John Chrysostom says in his *Homilies on Hebrews*,

---

1. Ephraim the Syrian, *Hymns and Homilies*.

"What then? Do we not offer [Christ's sacrifice] daily? Yes we offer, but making remembrance of His death" (17, 3 [6]).[2]

So the question to be answered is, "Was the morsel in John 13: 26–27 a valid communion?" As for readers of the biblical canon after its formation, John's readers have also read in Luke's gospel the following: "Then he took a loaf of bread, and when he had given thanks, he broke it and gave it to them, saying, 'This is my body, which is given for you. Do this in remembrance of me.' And he did the same with the cup after supper, saying, 'This cup that is poured out for you is the new covenant in my blood. But see, the one who betrays me is with me, and his hand is on the table. For the Son of Man is going as it has been determined, but woe to that one by whom he is betrayed!' Then they began to ask one another which one of them it could be who would do this" (22:19–23).

Is this not, in its beginning lines, an establishment of the Eucharistic institution? And is it not followed by the *expectation* of Judas' betrayal? "Behold, the hand of him who betrays me is with me on the table" clearly says Judas is still there. Of course the accounts by Luke and John differ, but the gospels differ in many respects. Just consider the differing accounts of Judas' suicide.

Kenneth D. Gangel gives his considered opinion on the Eucharist as follows, "The flesh and blood are spiritual realities in our appropriation of the power of the cross." "Spiritual realities" and "power of the cross" are perfectly in keeping with my position.[3]

N. T. Wright, in his *John for Everyone,* apparently has 13:26–27 in mind when he writes, "Now Jesus is back in Jerusalem for a final Passover. John does not describe the meal itself; presumably he supposes that his readers know the story of it well enough from other traditions, and from the experience of the Eucharist"[4]

And in Wright's *New Testament and the People of God* he has elaborated further on this. "The fact that Paul can chide his congregation in Corinth for their misbehavior at the Eucharist shows that this celebratory meal was so inbuilt into the structure of early

2. Ephraim the Syrian, *Hymns and Homilies.*
3. Gangel, *Ministering to Today's Adults.*
4. Wright, *John for Everyone,* 44.

Christianity that even within a very early congregation it could be taken for granted and abused" So much for Clarke's "utter mistake."[5]

What's more, the Anglican *Book of Common Prayer* evidently agrees: But if we are to share rightly in the celebration of those holy Mysteries,[6] and be nourished by that holy Food, we must remember the dignity of that holy Sacrament. I therefore call upon you to consider how Saint Paul exhorts all persons to prepare themselves carefully before eating of that Bread and drinking of that Cup. For, as the benefit is great, if with penitent hearts and living faith we receive the holy Sacrament, so is the danger great, if we receive it improperly, not recognizing the Lord's Body. "Judge yourselves, therefore, lest you be judged by the Lord." Now if Jesus's action in John 13: 26–27 is understood to be the Eucharist (which at this point seems more than likely), why does Satan enter him rather than the body and blood of Christ? I am personally convinced that it has to do with the words in Luke 22:19 (and in 1 Cor 11:23–26), spoken after the breaking of bread at the Last Supper: "Do this in remembrance of Me." The Greek word that is translated "remembrance" is *anamnesin,* which can also be translated "call to mind."

Coming as the memorial sentence does, immediately after His having identified the elements with his body and blood, it is reasonable to see this passage as referring to a good or spiritually healthy communion. And if that is so, then what can Judas's communion be except an evil or poisonous one, with Satan entering him instead of Christ's body and blood?

What we apparently find in the Eucharist then is a specific physical act which opens a door of our souls to something spiritual. If Jesus is called to mind in gratitude during the action, it is His essence, his strength, and his life that enters; whereas if we are unbelieving at that moment, it is evil that enters. The choice lies in the communicant's thoughts and emotions being appropriate to the source and person behind the act, and not to something opposed and extraneous to them.

---

5. Wright, *New Testament and the People of God.*

6. Wood, *Book of Common Prayer.*

And in the context of John 13: 26–28, Judas' betrayal of Jesus indicates that this is key to the passage. In all probability, Judas was thinking of the thirty pieces of silver he would make by selling his Lord to the Sanhedrin. Hence an ancient act of special friendship (the morsel) is returned as an act of betrayal and enmity. In support of this probability, I offer the following two items: John tells of Judas stealing from the money he carried on behalf of his fellow disciples, an indication of his constantly thinking of money. Yet another would be his wily comment after the woman poured expensive nard over Jesus' feet, words to the effect that the nard's value could have gone to the poor, while, as the evangelist tells us, the truth was that he personally would benefit from the year's wages he was promised for betraying Jesus. Here we can see Judas' inclination to prefer the worldly value of money over a spiritual action that prefigured Jesus' death and burial.

In support of my attempt to suggest a more orderly mind when receiving communion, I cite 1 Corinthians 11:21–22. Here Paul admonishes the Corinthian church for its waywardness during communion. "For when it is time to eat, everyone proceeds with his own supper. One is hungry and another becomes drunk. . .. Are you trying to show contempt for the church of God?. . .. I will not praise you for this."

Admittedly this reprimand was based on behavior in the early church's meeting to eat an entire meal in someone's private home, but the principle holds true today. The communicants were thinking only of themselves, their hunger for earthly food and their ruinous lust for overdrinking wine, not on Christ's having established the meal in order to carry the beneficial effects of his life and death down through the ages. If this were not so, there would be no need for Paul to chastise the Christian who was hungry.

And finally, let's recall Jesus' earlier accusation aimed at the 5,000, whose feeding is recorded in John 6:16–19: "You are looking for me not because you saw miraculous signs, but because you ate all the loaves of bread you wanted. Do not work for the food that disappears, but for the food that remains to eternal life—the food which the Son of Man will give to you." In this instance, the error committed is not from a complete lack of regard for Jesus, but from their lack of thought given to the sanctity of the miraculous multiplication of bread. They see Jesus as a candidate for kingship, but not as the Son of God who wishes to bless them with eternal life.

Again and again people forget the extreme importance of what communion represents and is. This is, I firmly believe, a mistake that has the potential to cancel or reverse any spiritual benefit in communion. It's just too easy for many Christian communicants throughout the world to ingest the bread and sip the wine while thinking, for example, of how inappropriate that woman's dress is, or how loud that bored toddler is being, or wondering if it's time to ask for a raise the next morning. I don't doubt they could repent and be forgiven, if only they knew the nature of their guilt. And their guilt is in thinking the physical act is enough while it is not.

While I am not prepared to discuss at any length the nature of Christ's presence in the elements, I do feel confident that it is altogether good for us to believe it is the Second Person of the Trinity who has promised that, in *some* real sense, his "body and blood" are in the elements for our ingestion—that is, as long as we are thinking gratefully toward Him while receiving—and grateful for his sacrifice on our behalf.

JUDEA AS DEATH IN
THE GOSPEL OF JOHN

I MUST BEGIN BY confessing that I agree with the doctrine that the mother of Jesus was not a virgin all her life. This seems clearly evident in, for example, Mark 3:32b: "Your mother and brothers are outside looking for you." As a result, I consider "James the brother of Jesus" was indeed his brother, as were several others.

In John's gospel, Jesus' brothers urge him to go to Judea, a place where "the Jews were looking for an opportunity to kill him" (7:1). While preparing this essay, I saw that no biblical exegete notices that the brothers' urgency for Jesus to go where "the Jews were looking for an opportunity to kill him" was an attempt to have Jesus killed.

In fact, after the brothers have been quoted as saying this, the evangelist writes, "For not even his brothers believed in him." Why would John make such a statement after quoting the brothers as saying, "No one who wants to be widely known acts in secret. . .. Show yourself to the world." These words, if read out of context, would tell us that the brothers are attempting to help Jesus to become more famous. But *in* context, we see that the brothers do not believe in him and wish to see him die.

The passage (7:1–9) nearly ends with Jesus saying, "My time has not yet fully come." The Greek word used for time here is *kairos*, a term, we are told, that refers to Jesus' death (and its aftermath). It seems the theory that says the brothers were slyly advising Jesus to go where He would lose his life is most probably valid when aptly understood.

This is the sort of passage we might find in a novel or short story written by an adept author writing today: a collection of hints rather than a bold statement. Perhaps that explains why Bible exegetes have not recognized the message it contains. My profession deals with the explication of literature, and John's writing certainly deserves to be seen within that category.

"SOMETHING UNDERSTOOD"

The Making of Christian Poetry in our Time

IN 1977 THE ANGLICAN Theological Review (ATR) conducted a survey of its subscribers, some results of which were (a) the discovery of a surprising lack of interest in the poetry section, and (b) a resultant hiatus in the publishing of poetry in ATR.

One important reason modern readers, whether professionals or not, do not read poetry is that our contemporaries tend to write poor poetry. This is to be expected if, as John Gardner tells us, "We are living, for all practical purposes, in an age of mediocre art." And Christian poetry is not exempt from this mediocrity.[1]

The importance of poetry to a culture has for centuries been a troubling question. Plato, we remember, wished poets banished from his Utopian republic; Aristotle defended them as effecting what he called *catharsis*. Considering that both philosophers were referring to all makers of imaginative literature, this has the look of a love-hate relationship with poetry when we notice that Plato, the attacker, is by far the more poetic in apprehension when he shapes his dialogues. This divided attitude manifested itself again in the next great flowering of literature in the Western Tradition: the Renaissance. In England, certain sincere sorts of men both condemned and praised poetry for its practical (moral) effects. Stephen Gosson, Anglican priest and sometime playwright, in his School of Abuse, traced the stages through which poetry takes the innocent,

1. Gardner, *On Moral Fiction*.

33

ending with sin, death and the devil.[2] Sir Philip Sidney, soldier, to whom School of Abuse was dedicated, responded with the Defense of Poesie in which he contradicts Gosson by maintaining that, by the "making" of feigned people and situations better than those commonly found in the world, the poet can encourage better living. In the Renaissance, as in classical Greece, probably too much is claimed by both sides. In nearly all cultures at all times, literate or not, there has been some kind of incantatory language (verse) just as there have been clothing and institutions. It seems a human constant. Verse gives pleasure to the speaking species.

But if the human kind is not only articulate but also, as an extension of speech, abstracting, imaging in the mind and with words things different from those present, and perhaps things more pleasant, then something beyond verse results; poetry. And perhaps because humans are intrinsically a moral species in potential (if C. S. Lewis is correct), but certainly because good art is always moral—that is, life-affirming—we sometimes have moral poetry and occasionally religious poetry.

But this as yet says nothing about the importance of poetry, only that it is common. The importance of poetry to a Christian, perhaps even to a theologian, lies in that ancient dispute between Plato and Aristotle, both of whom were right. The poet is, in one sense, mad; he thinks on the edge of human commonplaces facing chaos, the yet-untamed, yet-irrational. His gift, if he has it, is to begin the long process of taming it to our minds, making it thinkable. If prayer, as George Herbert wrote, is both a "plummet sounding heav'n and earth" and "something understood" (among other things), so is poetry.[3] The poet, if he has integrity of mission as a poet, does not indulge himself in hidden meanings, at least not in making them more hidden than they were; he exerts his force in the other direction. As Owen Barfield has said, "You cannot make poetry by cunningly removing all the clues which, if left, would discover the stale-ness of your meaning. " The poet, he later adds, "must talk what is nonsense on the face of it [because of the nature

2. Gosson, *School of Abuse.*

3. Herbert, *Complete Poetry.*

of his new meaning], but in such a way that the recipient may have the new meaning suggested to him."[4] This is the true importance of metaphor, the lifeblood of poetry. If Plato focused upon the chaotic part of the poetic process, the dangerous part, Aristotle focused on the salutary part, the successes, in speaking of poetry's purging one of pity and fear: fear, I suspect, of the chaos, pity for the protagonist who faces it, the persona of the poet. Sophocles was a little mad to write *Oedipus Tyrranos*, but his brush with madness brought incest, hatred of authority, and the fate vs. freewill paradox just inside thought from a wilderness of mere emotions.

Such talk of chaos is reminiscent of what Fredrick Holmgren has said regarding proverbial wisdom and Job. One of Holmgren's points is that theology matures and is renewed by facing facts of life for which it did not formerly account, facts such as those which the book of Job faces and begins to assimilate. It is also reminiscent of what Urban T. Holmes writes regarding theology and religious renewal, that "genuine renewal . . . requires us to move, at times, to the edge of chaos."

There is of course a difference between renewal by "recovery of Christian tradition," as this journal describes it on its frontispiece, and renewal by expanding the frontiers of theology. I would imagine that both could aptly be called renewal. But since I am not a theologian and cannot always distinguish the new from the recovered, and since the distinction does not affect my thesis, I will ignore it, calling all of the burden of live metaphors "recovered meaning. " At any rate this suits the case of the Christian poet better than "new meaning," which might better apply to mystical poets, who may or may not be Christian.

At this point I can imagine being asked what became of originality as a criterion for the appreciation and judging of poetry. If the Christian poet is expected only to recapture old meanings, how can he say anything fresh and strong? How can he be creating anything he can truly call his own? It is the attitude toward art underlying such questions which has, in great part, caused much twentieth-century poetry to be such rude and feeble fare as to be

---

4. Barfield, *Importance of Language.*

wholesomely ignored. If humans are capable of originality at all, it is certainly a far more rare and difficult achievement than the number of "original" poems published every year would indicate. Far offener, mere crudity of sentiment, or gratuitous conflict, or even an athletic typography, are pressed into service and made to pass for originality. Furthermore, to equate "old meanings" with staleness and weakness is not only to betray a confusion of ideas with material bodies and a prejudice against maturity, it also betrays an ignorance of the relationship between decaying language and the tendency of meanings to leak from words as those words decay in heavy use. The meanings survive in potential to be caught again by newly crafted words, just as the clear rain water someone catches today and drinks from a glass is the same water Diogenes of Sinope drank from his hands and then urinated into the marketplace. If we refuse to drink liquids on that account, we do so on pain of dessication. For the Christian at least, it is difficult to see how anything can be held as entirely one's own.

My purpose in this essay is not to excoriate weak Christian verse, nor even to define good Christian verse. But if verse can be anything more than what Horace called *dulce*, if it can also be, in some sense, *utile*, then surely verse by Christian poets has both the opportunity and the cause to be so. My point is that good poetry is both beautiful and (in some sense) true, that good poetry is written by poets who are both skillful and wise. The ideal poet is a skillful versifier with wisdom. Lacking any other source of wisdom (divine inspiration, for example), the poet can do little better than to draw upon the wisdom of Christianity. As Cicero said of the orator, "No one can be eloquent on a matter he knows nothing about," and "Even if he does know the subject to perfection, he can still only speak eloquently about it if he knows how to dress his remarks in an attractive style."[5] In most good poets, the two are synthesized. In too many poets writing today, they are not.

There appear to be several reasons for this. For one thing, our culture is not at all sure that it wants wisdom. Few of us enjoy being lectured at. But good poems are hardly ever lectures. If I have given

5. Cicero, *On the Good Life.*

the impression that what is needed are verse homilies, it is time I corrected the error. It is also time I gave an example of good poetry, ancient or modern, Christian or secular. C. S. Lewis's little-known epigram will do:

> All things (e.g. a earners journey through
> A needle's eye) are possible, it's true.
> But picture how the camel feels, squeezed out
> In one long bloody thread from tail to snout.

There is no modern reveling here in the surrealism of the image for its own sake, the extruded, painful and transmogrified animal. It is clearly a poem about a love of earthly riches and the incompatibility of such love with the way of Christ, yet the abstract and literal statement is as absent here as it was from Christ's own parables. Indeed the poem derives the only valuable meaning it can have from the corresponding incident and dominical simile in the synoptic Gospels. Even where it seems at first glance to depart from the gospel account in affirming the possibility of the rich man's salvation, this apparent departure is couched in an English phrase which often carries a sense of the next-to-impossible: "All things are possible, it's true." The force of the poem lies in the scriptural direction, reinvigorating the gospels' sense of extreme difficulty for such cases. This is synthesis of versification skills (about which I have said nothing yet) with wisdom. It would be hard to classify it a great poem, but it is more satisfactory in effect than many longer poems being written today. This is not to say that good poetry can never make a statement. It can, especially if it bases its statements upon—and laces them with— images of specifics, as W. H. Auden's "Musée des Beaux Arts" does:

> About suffering they were never wrong,
> The Old Masters: how well they understood
> Its human position; how it takes place
> While someone else is eating or opening a window or
> just walking dully along;
> How, when the aged are reverently, passionately waiting
> For the miraculous birth, there always must be
> Children who did not specially want it to happen, skating

On a pond at the edge of the wood:
They never forgot
That even the dreadful martyrdom must run its course
Anyhow in a corner, some untidy spot
Where the dogs go on with their doggy life and the
torturer's horse
Scratches its innocent behind on a tree.

In Breughel's Icarus, for instance: how everything turns
away
Quite leisurely from the disaster; the ploughman may
Have heard the splash, the forsaken cry,
But for him it was not an important failure; the sun shone
As it had to on the white legs disappearing into the green
Water; and the expensive delicate ship that must have
seen
Something amazing, a boy falling out of the sky,
Had somewhere to get to and sailed calmly on.[6]

To say that Christians all too easily think, with the benefits of hindsight, that if they had been in Jesus' presence, or present at a martyrdom, they would have acted with a becoming piety at every moment, given full attention, recognized the situation for its full importance; to say that this would not inevitably have been true is wisdom, and the poem does say something like this. But merely to say this is not to write poetry, as Auden well knew. He even goes beyond simply inserting a concrete image here and there between statements. His statements draw life from the facts of those dull and mechanical acts with which people have always filled their lives, necessary acts for a material existence of course, but less important and tending always to displace more important acts. The first verse paragraph contains what explicit statement the poem makes, while at the turn all becomes focused on the unified scenario of Breughel's painting and the Icarus myth: both the "miraculous birth" and the "dreadful martyrdom" become chronologically collapsed into "a boy falling out of the sky" to his death, the most miraculous birth out of millions as it was the most dreadful martyrdom. Though the poem's statements function vitally, they recover no meanings lost; it

6. Auden, *Collected Poems.*

is in fact highly debatable whether the master painters, as a group, understood human suffering any better than several other groups one might name. It is in the illustrations of the first paragraph—the opening of the window, the skating children—that the reader is brought near the edge of the expectable. The reader has, presumably, experienced the dogginess of dogs sniffing the ground at a trot or nosing one another's behinds, and has, again presumably, felt occasionally the incongruity and absurdity of such trivial and quotidian events blindly continuing when something life-shattering is going on nearby. It moves one to the edge of the expectable by taking one out of the customary mind-set of the poetry reader and into the alertness necessary in meeting the events of "real" life.

And then the poem moves into its final paragraph, which creates the great metaphor using Breughel's painting of the Icarus disaster. Here nouns and verbs do not connect in mechanical simplicity with things and actions as they do in literal statements. Here, instead, we are given a "splash" to mark a point somewhere near Christ's death; here the "white legs disappearing" are upside-down. But they are recognizable as or at least akin to those upright white legs which one imagines at eye level on the cross; the "forsaken cry" is recollectible; and the phrase "a boy falling out of the sky" is an oddly effective offhand way of referring to Christ's advent and death without referring to them at all. The poem is not precisely "about Jesus Christ" because it never looks directly at him. It looks beside him at something different but related. As with peripheral vision, it looks to one side of the object in order to see the object more clearly. By so doing, the poem recovers a poignant sense of human unpreparedness for truly important events, perhaps a sense even of human unworthiness of such events as the incarnation and redemption. The poem stands on the firm ground of tame everyday events and gazes steadily at a wild thought, wild but wise and worthy of recovery.

At the tamer end of the spectrum of good Christian verse, there are hymns like the one by Isaac Watts, "When I survey the wondrous cross. . . ," If Auden's poem recovers some meaning related to the incarnation and crucifixion, Watts' lyrics proceed through some of the same meanings of Christ's sacrifice one might hear any Sunday in a careful homily on Galatians 6:14. This is excellent Augustan hymnody, and remains excellent today as hymnody. But it edges toward failure as hymnody in the third stanza where it is at its best as poetry. In two tetrameter lines, Watts not only envisions Christ's love as united with his sorrows, but he also sees them fused in Christ's blood. This goes beyond the easily received and immediately comprehensible. In going so far it strains the limitations of hymnody: the listener who is caught in the dynamics of ceremony has no time to stop, reflect, and understand. It goes very near—though it does not quite come to—violation of Watts' own stated criteria for his verse: "I have thrown out the Lines that were too sonorous and have giv'n an allay to the Verse, lest a more exalted Turn of Thought or Language should darken or disturb the Devotion of the plainest Souls."[7]

Some of the lines Watts "threw out" were the original fourth stanza of "When I survey":

> His dying crimson, like a robe,
> Spreads o'er his body on the tree;
> Then am I dead to all the globe,
> And all the globe is dead to me.[8]

This stanza was marked for deletion by Watts. He was judicious in this, for the omitted stanza, which originally followed the one discussed above, carried the image of Christ's blood into even more daring poetry. Here the worshiper is faced immediately with an unsettling pun upon "dying" (unsettling especially for the eighteenth century): Christ's "crimson" (blood) is both concomitant to his act of ceasing life (dying) and, more and more as it flows, the blood is coloring (dyeing) him crimson. It is as if the worshiper were being spoken to by two people simultaneously; he must have a moment of quiet from them in order to sort out the two apparently different statements.

Perceiving an interchangeability between ceasing life and altering hue is not so easy as to be instantaneous. Once one relates, however, the simile of the crimson "robe" with the crown of thorns

---

7. Bond, *Poetic Wonder of Isaac Watts*.

8. Bond, *Poetic Wonder of Isaac Watts*.

in the preceding stanza, one begins to understand that the description is of Christ suddenly revealed on the cross to be royal, as signified by the color and the appurtenance of royal prerogative. But the crimson robe at least was not of the sort one gains by human means—that is to say by intentional and political means—government. It was not an external and artificial robe but rather an internal and genuine one, wholly intrinsic in the wearer. In this rejection of him by the world then, in the immediate cause of the blood, there is implicit his superiority over the world. Once Watt has reached this point, he is ready to paraphrase what was part of his targeted passage in Galatians: "the cross of our Lord Jesus Christ, by whom the world is crucified unto me, and I unto the world." The revelation of Christ as true King causes then so total a reorientation that it may be spoken of as crucifixion of the self—or of the world. "The world, then, and all its pursuits—the cargoes of "expensive delicate ships," the ships themselves, ploughmen, scratching horses, all of the dogs in their doggy activities—are rejected in Watts' hymn by virtue of a vision of Someone far more important than this world.

Now it may be seen that this hymn takes a point of view almost diametrically the opposite of Auden's poem. Even in the most cerebral, symbolic and suggestive passage of Watts' hymn, the attitude is one of a vision of Christ's having blinded the speaker to the natural world, whereas in Auden's poem the attitude is of the world languidly ignoring the "amazing" new fact of self-sacrifice. In his clean sweep of the natural world's ignorance of this fact, Auden even includes the sun, contradicting the account of darkness at the crucifixion in the Synoptics. Watts' verses keep well within the well-trod grounds of Christian piety, while Auden's poem ventures so far beyond those grounds that a reader of delicate piety might be offended by some of his implications.

What I have marked out by these two examples of good Christian verse are two extremes between which I believe a faithful but also open-eyed and live Christian verse may serve well the present Christian community. To quote from Lord David Cecil's perceptions on the weakness of much Christian verse:

> The Hebrew psalmists . . . spill themselves without shame
> in their invocations to God; show themselves rancorous
> or self-pitying or boastful just as the mood dictates. Their
> mode of expressing themselves is equally uninhibited.
> "The Lord awaked out of sleep like a giant refreshed with
> wine"; no devotional writer of later days would permit
> himself to use such an image about the All-holy, All-wise
> object of his adoration. The New Testament conception
> of God is so much more elevated than that of the Old
> that the devout person feels it profane to show himself
> in all his earthy imperfections before Him. He will al-
> low himself to express only unexceptionable sentiments,
> love, reverence, humility: will voice no aspiration save
> for a purer soul and stronger faith. As for using any but
> the most decorous language to express his feelings, the
> very idea horrifies him. Now very few people live at a suf-
> ficiently high moral level to find it natural to express only
> virtuous sentiments and in the language of impeccable
> taste, with the consequence that much Christian verse
> is, by an aesthetic standard, insincere. The writer, that is,
> does not say what he really feels, but what he thinks he
> ought to feel: and he speaks not in his own voice but in
> the solemn tones that seem fitting to his solemn subject.[9]

Cecil is not thinking of Watts when he sketches the timorous
end of the spectrum of Christian verse—a few pages along he
praises the sentiment and lyricism of Watts' best hymns—but the
points he fixes of spontaneity and then timidity lie along the same
line as the spectrum I am describing. As further clarification of this
line of gradations, there is at its timorous end such Christian verse
as repeats certain key words of Christian doctrine while taking for
granted both feeling and belief in the reader. At the opposite end lie
such poems as, for example,

> the angels sang in harmony, relief was the sigh
> no more burdened hearts, with the unequal cry
> equality had been found, a blessing from above
> the day the world found out, there was no colour in love[10]

9. Cecil, *Poets and Story-tellers.*

10. Cecil, *Poets and Story-tellers.*

Within these far extremes and set in from them, lie such poems as "When I survey" and "Musée des Beaux Arts," neither taking belief totally for granted nor grievously contradicting orthodox Christian belief. And at an even more central position, at the midmost point on this continuum, lie such poems as George Herbert wrote. Within a broad via media here, the poem can be more courageous than the hymn meant for congregational singing, but yet not so recklessly adventuresome into unassimilated matters as to limit its audience severely. For convenience' sake we may call poems like Auden's, the poetry of pagan mythology, the poetry of waters (nearby, the poetry of the sea: the inchoate); very venturesome Christian verse, often art as great as any in the language, but somewhat limited in audience. More orthodox yet, but still extremely vigorous, are such Old Testament poems as the Psalms, the poetry of wine by which the reader may either "reel" or "shout" with recovered vigor. Still moving in the tamer direction, we come to Herbert and the poetry of bread, poetry to the New Testament view of God with much of the Old Testament earthiness, poetry on a human scale but imbued with divine meaning extracted from chaos to the sight. Even here poetry is not tamed enough for hymnody. That is next and tamer, the poetry of sounds more than things, words with meanings so customary that they will not disturb the devotion of any worshiper. Last, and also least, is the tamest of all the poetry of (more or less) pure sound, words which depend for their pathetic effect upon the absence of meaning; this is poetry which pulls such words as "love," "faith," and "joy" off the shelf of Christian vocabulary and tosses them together disrespectfully into something approaching angel food cake, tasteful only to those few with an unregenerate sweet tooth, and often decaying into cynicism. It would have as restricted an audience as the wildest, most chaotic poetry published except that it requires less work to pervert one's taste to it.

But to leave the extremes to those who might profit from them, I return to the via media and the likes of Herbert. Here is a brief selection of stanzas from his long poem, "The Sacrifice":

> Oh all ye, who passe by, whose eyes and minde
> To worldly things are sharp, but to me blinde;

To me, who took eyes that I might you finde:
Was ever grief like mine?
The Princes of my people make a head
Against their Maker: they do wish me dead,
Who cannot wish, except I give them bread:
Was ever grief like mine? . . .
Then with a scarlet robe they me aray;
Which shews my bloud to be the onely way
And cordiali left to repair mans decay:
Was ever grief like mine?
Then on my head a crown of thorns I wear:
For these are all the grapes Sion doth bear,
Though I my vine planted and watred there:
Was ever grief like mine? . . .
But, O my God, my God! why leav'st thou me,
The sonne, in whom thou dost delight to be?
My God, my God—
Never was grief like mine.[11]

In these few lines of verse are several phrases one may use to take a fix on the centrality of such Christian verse. Like Watts', the poem takes Christ's crucifixion as its subject; like Auden's, it recovers meaning in the self-sacrifice. Like Watts', it presents no doctrine offensive to the orthodox; again like Auden's, it revivifies doctrine by unabashedly looking at the tangible facts of life. This is akin to, but is not, a hymn; it could be sung in churches, but the time it requires for understanding, and for the resulting emotional response, would make public worship halting and awkward. It is a poem to be read and savored by one in a private room with the door shut. And yet, with all of the intellectual force that has gone into the making of it, Herbert has not made it accessible only to intellectuals.

Like Watts' and Auden's poems, it touches on the question of the world's cognizance of the self-sacrifice. But where Watts made his hymn more comfortable by using the first-person singular for the observer, thereby allowing himself the feasibility of one exceptional person's recognizing so much import in the crucifixion (along with the advantage of hindsight in the modern worshiper's identifying with the "I" of the poem), Herbert uses the first-person

11. Herbert, *Works*, 26–33,

singular for the crucified Christ, forcing his poem to be contemporaneous and unflinching in the face of discomfiting facts. And where Auden's poem depicts painfully exaggerated ignorance on the part of witnesses, Herbert exerts his gift to mend the ignorance of his reader.

Being relatively free of the constraints of hymnody, Herbert can keep intact the conceit of the mocking scarlet robe as fused with Christ's redeeming blood. He can even indulge reverently in the pun on "cordiali," indicating that the blood both comes from the heart and acts as medicine for sin. Far from seeing the crown of thorns as "rich," Herbert confronts squarely the pain of their fruitlessness. And unlike Auden's poem, Herbert's is explicitly Christian, allowing him to refer explicitly to the robe and crown, and to deal with them straightforwardly and in detail.

I have selected these poems for their comparability but I do not intend to imply that all Christian poetry of the via media deals with the crucifixion. Still within the limits of these loose boundaries, slightly less assimilated than Herbert's but not so painfully stark as Auden's, is a recent poem by John Berryman, the first of "Eleven Addresses to the Lord":

> Master of beauty, craftsman of the snowflake,
> inimitable contriver,
> endower of Earth so gorgeous & different from the boring
> Moon, thank you for such as it is my gift.
> I have made up a morning prayer to you
> containing with precision everything that most matters.
> 'According to Thy will' the thing begins.
> It took me off & on two days. It does not aim at
> eloquence.
> You have come to my rescue again & again in my impassable, sometimes
> despairing years. You have allowed my brilliant friends to destroy
> themselves and I am still here, severely damaged, but functioning.
> Unknowable, as I am unknown to my guinea pigs:
> how can I 'love' you?

> I only as far as gratitude & awe
> confidently & absolutely go.
> I have no idea whether we live again.
> It doesn't seem likely
> from either the scientific or the philosophical point
> of view but certainly all things are possible to you,
> and I believe as fixedly in the Resurrection-appearances
> to Peter & to Paul as I believe I sit in this blue chair. Only
> that
> may have been a special case to establish their initiatory
> faith.
> Whatever your end may be, accept my amazement. May
> I stand until death forever
> at attention for any your least instruction or enlighten-
> ment. I even feel sure you will
> assist me again, Master of insight & beauty.[12]

Intelligible but thought-packed, honest yet devout; alert in every line to what he knows and does not know, humble even in his knowledge, dignified in his ignorance, the poet demonstrates as well here as any poet I know that Christian verse in our time need be informed with neither unintelligent optimism nor academic ennui; that it need not, on the one hand tread exclusively the known rounds of Christian doctrine, nor fling itself and the reader with reckless abandon into unknown and dimly perceived matters.

There is a place for good hymnody as there is a place for mystical or oracular utterances. But there is a place for good central Christian poetry too, and it is neither in congregational singing nor the dark waters of public oblivion. It is before the eyes of living, literate humans.

---

12. Berryman, *Love and Fame.*

AN INTRODUCTION
TO ACTED PARABLES
IN THE GOSPELS

ON MORE THAN ONE occasion, the disciples of Jesus do not understand his parables. Occasionally they will ask him for an explanation of his latest, and at least once he replies with some surprise that after hearing so many, and with the scripture so familiar to them, they still must have things explained to them: Beginning in Mark 7:17 we read "His disciples asked him about the parable. And he said to them, 'Then are you also without understanding? Do you not see that. . .'" In John 10:6, when Jesus has told them the parable of the good shepherd, the evangelist says, "But they did not understand what he was saying to them," so Jesus explains this too, a sure indication that the message is important.

But if the meanings of the spoken parables are important for Christians to understand, then we may suppose that acted parables are important as well. And our supposition is strongly supported when, in John 13:7, as he approaches Peter to wash his feet, and the apostle tries to refuse the honor, Jesus says to him, "What I am doing you do not understand now, but afterward you will understand." Then after washing all of his disciples' feet, the Lord asks them, "Do you understand what I have done to you?" The disciples do not understand much of what Jesus tells them, and they are visibly frustrated by his speaking in figurative terms, for later on they say to him, "Ah, now you are speaking plainly and not using figurative speech!"

The disciples are not stupid, but they are unaccustomed to metaphoric speech. They expect everyone to "speak plainly," just as we do in our time. But Jesus does not stop using parabolic language (and actions) until he is near the end of his earthly life. He evidently considered it an important way for Christians to think. And how can we, if we consider ourselves Christians, disagree with him? How can we not make a sincere effort to accustom ourselves to this mode of communication when the Communicator is so central to our lives, a Communicator who Paul says has literally "emptied" himself in order to take on a form in which he could communicate with us?

People who know the ways of animals recognize what a dog means when it holds its tail tucked between its legs. They know the dog is saying, "You're the boss. I'm your humble servant." That signal has been known for centuries. More recently people have realized that horses too use body language. A horse with ears laid back is expressing anger or fear, while its tail held high speaks of excitement or dominance. A gorilla staring directly in your face is challenging or warning you, and this same animal will interpret your stares at him in the same way.

These animals at times will also use sounds to communicate. A dog will whine or bark, a horse will whinny, a gorilla will utter pig-like grunts while foraging. But sounds are not their primary way of communicating. Body language is.

We humans have reversed the emphasis. When we have something to say, we usually say it with our vocal cords. But we use body language as well. We may nod instead of saying the word "yes." To abruptly leave a meeting at a crucial point in the discussion, or to turn and walk away from a private conversation without the appropriate remarks, expresses sharp disagreement. The military salute is an expression of solidarity and respect: "I carry no weapons against you." A wink can mean, "We know the secret, don't we?" A discreet kick under the table by a spouse often means, "Watch out. You're saying too much." A handshake (of the conventional kind) says, "Polite respect," while a different handshake (more elaborate) says, "We're members of the same covert group—allies." Body language, while it is at least as old as the species *homo sapiens,* is a form humans have come to rely on less and less as we have come to make finer distinctions among meanings.

However, except for sophisticated forms of sign language, what people generally call body language tends to express the signer's emotion rather than communicating a more informative message. That is to say, the popular conception of "body language" is not developed much beyond the flattened ears of horses and the tucked tails of dogs I mentioned earlier. We are told, for example, that a person's "sitting with legs crossed, foot kicking slightly," is to be interpreted as boredom, while "tapping or drumming fingers" means impatience.

But there is a more complex form of body language that goes by another name; it is called demonstration, something we use in teaching almost without realizing we are doing it. Try to imagine learning to cook from a radio program or CD, and you will soon realize why cooking programs are so popular on television. We watch the chef adding the herbs by rubbing them between her hands, or we watch him remove the bones from a chicken, and the image of a human being, performing the act we would like to perform for ourselves, becomes more natural to us. The popular saying that "a picture is worth a thousand words" does not go quite far enough. Some things can be communicated fully only by images, only by watching, only by imitating. No number of words can substitute for seeing something done. A teacher's demonstrations can communicate far more than a single emotion. An adult can show a youngster how to chop a log with an axe, with or without accompanying words. An observant young person will understand that the feet should be spaced the width of the shoulders; that the left hand should hold the end of the handle, while the right hand grips the handle much higher, nearer the head; that one's torso is upright at the top of the stroke, then bends downward as the axe descends; and that the right hand should slide down the handle to meet the left hand as the axe makes contact with the log. All of this is learnable from less than a second of body motion. Verbal descriptions can leave us confused, but a demonstration can cut through the verbiage and allow us to do what primates do best—imitate. And as a valuable bonus, demonstrations (especially when followed by the learner's practicing) are much more *memorable* than verbal descriptions for most of us.

And then, when sincerity is an issue, sincere concern, genuine affection, we enjoy the physical form of message. Letters are welcome (even the electronic variety), cards are delightful, and telephone calls are appreciated, but none of these means of communication says, "I love you" or "I want you to get well" as effectively as a visit.

Jesus Christ visited us. He showed up in bodily form. I point this out, not merely to indicate the sincerity of God's concern for us, but mostly in order to bring up the added medium of Christ's body for his communicating with us. He could of course communicate vocally and did, but he also moved about with his body; slept on a boat; drank water and wine; ate fish, bread, and most probably lamb; wore clothes; gathered the dust of the road on his feet; formed a whip of cords; climbed hills; and allowed his body to be beaten and then nailed to a wooden structure in the shape of a cross. Of *course* these displayed his concern for us and for our salvation. Of *course* his descent from heaven to the inconveniences and tortures of earth inspires awe in us for his acceptance of the humiliation it was. But it is seldom recognized that his taking upon himself this self-soiling thing we call a body also afforded him the means of speaking through body language. But the body language we speak of now goes even beyond demonstration on occasion. It becomes parable—*acted* parable.

In some ways, Jesus' actions were like this for people in his day. They heard his words, and they saw his meaningful actions, but the message he brought to them was one they had not encountered: He would die and then live; they would do something similar; he was authorized to forgive sins on behalf of God; Jews were not automatically better people than non-Jews; and so on. But as Christian readers of the gospels today, our difficulty is different: We know the basics of his message (at least we know them cognitively); what most of us are unfamiliar with is this non-verbal way of conveying meanings. We generally read the gospels for their verbal lessons; when we come to the passages describing Jesus' actions, we are usually content to see them only as records of actual events.

And the fact that many of these events do not seem choreographed by Jesus lends support to the impression that they are random and meaningless. Perhaps at such moments we temporarily put aside our belief that Jesus was the Son of God and was constantly cooperating with the will of the Father, who, at his discretion, is able to control all things.

We may also suffer from a lack of intimate familiarity with Old Testament habits and traditions. Ezekiel 15 tells the parable of the vine wood, chapter 17 tells the parable of the two eagles, and Nathan's parable to David is famous, but these are spoken parables. The Old Testament holds acted parables as well: Nehemiah's shaking out the front of his garment, an action symbolizing God's shaking out every man from his house who does not fulfill the promise to return the property and the interest payments of fellow Jews who are in debt; Isaiah's going naked and barefoot for three years as a symbol of the captive status of Egypt and Assyria to come. Parables of action are more a part of the Old Testament tradition than are spoken parables, so it should surprise no one that Jesus used both. And if the unanimity of Old Testament acted parables is any guide, we may take it as a rule that Jesus' acted parables were all designed and commanded by the Father. And there are many others like these.

We all know of the feeding of thousands of men (to say nothing of women and children) on only a few loaves of bread and a couple of fish, but we don't always realize that one important meaning of this parable is that, in our working for Christ (assuming always that we are doing our utmost), our small acts are magnified by the Father so as to accomplish great things.

And then when Jesus walks on the water, his contemporaries among the Jews would have seen that act alone as his having power to tame chaos, for they saw the sea as chaotic. And when Peter tries to imitate his master, he succeeds only as long as he keeps his eyes on Jesus beyond him. But as soon as Peter looks down at the chaotic waves, he begins to sink. Clearly when the going feels hopeless, we have to keep our mind's eye on Jesus who alone can teach us to walk safely through a seemingly chaotic world.

And a final example is the lowering of a paralytic man down through a hole in the roof to be healed. There are several things to be said about this acted parable, but the one that is most important to us in our time is that access to God is not always complete for everyone through traditional channels alone. We must also seek God in private prayer, as well as changing our lifestyle so as to come closer to that of Jesus.

None of these will become part of our lives immediately, but if we recognize and remember these lessons, they will become part of us and seemingly ease our burdens. And we will remember them more easily because actions are easier to remember than lessons we are taught in words. Jesus knew this. He was the consummate teacher.

THE TRINITY

LET'S BEGIN BY LAYING down a basic ground rule. Let's recognize the fact that the word "Lord" in the mouths of the earliest Christians *meant* God. You can see this in Isaiah 44:6, "This is what the Lord says—Israel's King and Redeemer, the Lord Almighty," a part of the book of Isaiah that may have been written as late as the second century B.C. It is not a basis for believing in the Trinity yet, but it prepares us for passages like 2 Corinthians 13:14—"May the grace of the Lord Jesus Christ, and the love of God, and the fellowship of the Holy Spirit be with you all." The latest date for this letter from Paul is 57 A.D., and some scholars date it even earlier. So only about twenty years after the crucifixion the apostle Paul is calling Jesus Christ God.

I cite this passage at my beginning for two reasons. (1) It is often referred to as a proof text for early belief in the Trinity, and (2) it demonstrates the importance placed on the divinity of Christ when Christians today are asked if they believe in the Trinity.

And by the way, if this already seems too scholarly, too much theology and not enough excitement, I will share with you a short passage from C.S. Lewis's book *Mere Christianity*. He writes, "If [someone] has once looked at the Atlantic [Ocean] from the beach, and then goes and looks at a *map* of the Atlantic, he will be turning from something real to something less real. . .. But the map is going to be of more use than walks on the beach if you want to get [from England] to America."[1]

1. Lewis, *Mere Christianity*.

So far so good. Then he goes on, "Theology is like the map. Merely learning and thinking about the Christian doctrines, if you stop there, is unreal and unexciting. Doctrines are not God: they are only a kind of map. But that map is based on the experience of hundreds of people who really were in touch with God."

And what are the clearest statements by the early church on the Trinity? The major creeds. In reading the one we recite nearly every Sunday, the Nicene Creed, we find, "We believe in *one God*, the Father, the Almighty. . ... We believe in *one Lord, Jesus Christ*. . ... We believe in the *Holy Spirit, the Lord*, the giver of life."

So where did this Nicene convention of early Christian clergy find support for their belief in the Trinity? In the Bible of course. So let's go through some of the New Testament passages that establish Christ's position as the Second Person of the Godhead. John 10:30 reads, in Christ's own words, "I and the Father are one." That needs no explanation. Then there is Matthew 1:23 in which the evangelist quotes Isaiah as saying, "The virgin will conceive and bear a son, and they will call him Immanuel, which means 'God with us.'" And in Colossians 2:9, Paul writes, "For in Christ all the fullness of the deity [that is, God] lives in bodily form."

In John 14:10 Jesus says to Philip, "Don't you believe that I am in the Father, and that the Father is in me?" Philippians 2:6-7 includes one of Paul's long sentences in support of Jesus being God: "[Jesus], being in true nature God, did not consider his equality with God [the Father] something to be used to his advantage, but *emptied* himself by taking the form of a servant, being made in human likeness." And this passage, by the way, explains why Jesus prays to God the Father asking for guidance, and why He says to his opponents who are about to stone him, "I have shown you many good works *from the Father*. For which of these will you stone me?" Here Jesus testifies clearly to his depending on the Father for his miracles, so how can He be God? Well, Paul explains this with the Greek word *kenosis;* Jesus went through an *emptying* of himself before his Incarnation. It was a temporary process, lasting thirty-three earthly years. Which is why He used a cushion to sleep on while the boat was tossing in a storm, why He was unable to heal some people in his home town, and why his prayer to have the bitter cup of crucifixion pass from him was refused. These examples, and a few others, have misled some people into doubting Christ's divinity, but the logic of the New Testament can solve their problem if they will listen to it.

And then, if we insist on it, there are passages establishing the divinity of the Holy Spirit. 2 Corinthians 3:17 says, "The Lord is the Spirit." That said, in order to keep this list of references to a minimum, I will quote only those from the gospels. Luke 1:35 quotes from the Annunciation to Mary, "The angel answered, 'The *Holy* Spirit will come upon you, and the power of the *Most High* will overshadow you.'" (This passage is patterned on Hebrew poetry, in which repetitions with a less important difference is the rule rather than meter and rhyme.) So "Holy Spirit" and "the Most High" have the same meaning; "Most High" *means* God the Father, so "Holy Spirit" also means God. Then there is Matthew 3:16–17, which reads, "As soon as Jesus was baptized, He rose up out of the water. At that moment heaven was opened, and He saw the *Spirit of God* descending like a dove and alighting on him. And a *voice from heaven said, 'This is my Son*, whom I love.'" Clearly the voice from heaven is the Father who is here identical with the Spirit of God.

Enough of citations. You get the idea: all three are God: Father, Son, and Holy Spirit. This has been examined and re-examined for two-thousand years, so there is no need to go over it again, except that many of us are satisfied with having seen the ocean from the beach, and therefore have not studied a map of it. But now that we have done so, we can look at the Trinity, not from God's point of view, but from our own position as human beings.

Because the written evidence is not the entire problem, our belief in the Trinity alone does not provide all of the evidence for belief. There must also be, in those who seek to truly believe, a preparation for belief. And that is what comes next. I think the major difficulty we have in accepting the three-in-one relationship of the Triune God is our lifelong earthly experience. The things around us strike us as naturally countable, so we assume each person is discrete—separate from every other human being. But when a man and woman marry and have a child, they are united in a way that baffles our understanding. We recite glibly that husband and wife are one body, but we don't understand what that means until we lose our spouse. Then we feel we have lost a part of ourselves, and we *have*. And the feeling is not much different when we lose a child.

In some mysterious way, our love for other people causes us to share our identity with them. So when we speak of mother, father and child, how many people are we thinking of? You might say *three*, but then if you hurt one of them, the other two react as if we have hurt them as well. And conversely if you do something helpful and unselfish for one of them, you can expect admiration from the other two in the nuclear family. So we could truly also say *one*. Do you see how we disbelieve in the countability of persons even in our everyday lives?

Now this is not meant to be a detailed picture of the Trinity. It is meant only to demonstrate that our unexamined idea of number is fallible, not to be trusted when we are speaking of heavenly reality. We cannot rely on instinct when we think about the one true Godhead and its three persons. They are at the same time one and three. Consider for a moment what is happening when we pray. We pray *to* God the Father, we are *motivated* to pray by the Holy Spirit inside us, and God the Son is the bridge along which we are being pushed to reach God.

If that seems difficult to understand, just think of it in this way. Christianity is not something people invented. If that were true, we could make it easier to understand. But God is not a human invention. We are trying to understand something that the human mind is not yet fully capable of understanding. That's why other religions seem so simple when compared with Christianity.

By this time I may be doing what some people call "beating a dead horse." But for some of us, for some imperishable human souls, the horse is far from dead. I think it would be safe to bet that most of us Christians today have recited the Nicene Creed without giving the words any more thought than to mouth those words. And what will we have for an answer then if someone on the edge of becoming a Christian asks us how we can believe in such an odd doctrine as three and one being the same substance? I have not given a complete answer to that question, but what I've given you is a starting point.

ARE SOME PEOPLE DOGS?

AS THE WORLD GROWS more fond of self-esteem, that phrase more often becomes a five-dollar term for plain old sinful pride. People gain esteem from the reputation of their faith, whatever the brand of faith, and will often go to extremes to refill the leaking self-esteem they gain from that association. High-school students react vehemently against their teachers' negative evaluation of their work, or against teachers' efforts at maintaining classroom discipline, for it lowers their self-esteem. It almost seems as if the people who believe most in their own inferiority react most hotly to being called inferior.

But not the Canaanite woman. When Jesus implies that she is like a dog compared with Jews, she does not deny his low social evaluation of her. In fact she seconds the motion by saying, "Even the dogs eat the scraps that fall from their master's table." Does she sound as if she needs a support group in self-assertion? Let me say that if she had had the dubious privilege of such a group, her daughter might not have been healed.

At this point we can use a little information on dogs in New Testament times. The word used in the original Greek *(kunariois)* could be, and has been translated as "little dogs," and that's not a bad translation except when it is understood to mean puppies. It refers to house dogs, as opposed to the half-wild dogs of the streets, which tended to be larger breeds. Think of the difference as miniature poodles and pekingeses as opposed to abandoned German shepherds and rotweilers running in packs and half-starved. Jesus does not use a word that means the larger, wilder type of dog. He means a family pet. When non-Jewish people ate their dinner, they threw the bones and other scraps on the floor, and the house-dogs cleaned up the mess. It worked for them.

Still, tame pet or not, he calls her a dog, and she accepts the slur he seemingly sees as the truth about her. *Seemingly* sees it as true, but actually the dialogue is a test of her faith, and she scores an A+. Even the apostles rarely receive such praise: "Your faith is strong." Make no mistake, if you and I make it through the pearly gates, Mrs. Canaanite will be a dazzling inhabitant of God's kingdom. We are not given her name, but she displays such faith by her persistence in prayers, and even in the event of insult, that she deserves our admiration.

Now why did Jesus test her so severely? I see two possibilities. One is that, in his state of *kenosis* (emptiness), this is the incident that triggered his realization that gentiles like us also were worthy in the Father's eyes. But this means this incident happened before such other interactions as he has with the Samaritan woman at the well, and the Roman soldier whose daughter he healed. And the problem with showing the likelihood of this is that the gospels don't usually stick to the order in which events happened. The evangelists are usually much more interested in grouping like lessons together than in preserving their chronological order, so we can't be sure which incident came first.

My own opinion is that he tests the Canaanite woman because too many people had trivialized his miracles. The day after a massive feeding on a miniscule amount of groceries, the crowd follows him to the opposite bank of the Sea of Galilee, not because they are in awe of the miracle and are grateful to God for it, but because their bellies are empty again. And when the rich young man asks Jesus what he must do to be saved, Jesus senses his pride in his wealth and tells him to give away everything he has and then follow him. The hungry crowd and the rich young man failed the test, but the Canaanite woman passed it because she truly believed Jesus was the Messiah of God ("son of David," she calls him) and therefore could enact miraculous cures, and because she wanted the healing for her daughter, not for herself. She withstands snubs and put-downs without retaliating in kind because she has only two things on her mind that day, the good of her beloved daughter, and the goodness of God.

She has self-esteem, yes. But her self-esteem, unlike that of many people, is generated and maintained within herself by her God-given strengths, one of which is motherly love, and another of which is her respect for God. It is not the fragile kind of self-esteem that depends on how others treat you, or speak to you, or even silently think about you. She asks insistently for the food that the Jewish people had thrown on the floor for the dogs to eat, and that food is the words and actions of God incarnate. In effect, she says to Jesus, "Your own people have rejected your generous blessings. May we foreigners not feed on what they have rejected?"

I love this unnamed Canaanite woman. May she be honored by the universal Christian church, for it is just possible, though we cannot prove it, that she was an instrument of God in his saving the whole world, and not just the "children of Israel." Let us call her St. Junia (Romans 16:7), for if anyone deserves to be called an apostle, she does.

But what can we learn from her for our own good? I believe she can teach us two spiritual lessons. The first is to realize, when we pray, that we are speaking to a living Being, not to a vending machine. There are Christians who rattle off their prayers without thinking of the meanings of the words. This happens to some of us with the Lord's Prayer. We seem to feel if we just say the correct words, God will take care of stuffing them with meaning. But the Canaanite woman will have nothing to do with this dropping of syllables like coins into a soda machine. She is persistent in her prayers, not for the sake of persistence itself, but because she aches for the restored health of her daughter. That's her first lesson for us; mean what you pray.

And the second is even harder to learn. I've already said that she takes no apparent offense at being called a house dog. What are we likely to be offended by? Have you ever been called old, if you are past a certain age, or called young if you want to do something only adults normally do? Either way, did it offend you? Maybe. Have you ever been asked the origin of your last name and considered the question racist? Perhaps. Has a salesperson ever implied that you could not afford something, and were you offended by the presumption, even if it's true? Has anyone ever referred to shameful acts in the past of your family, your denomination, or of the Christian church, thereby offending you? Leaving illegitimate births and unfaithful parents aside, did someone refer to the infamous Western Church's abandonment of the Eastern Church when the Turks attacked Constantinople, and so offended you?

Even if none of these specific things have happened to you, ask yourself what actions of others have offended you in the past. In fact, does this essay offend you? If so, now ask yourself if you are too easily offended. I ask myself this question almost daily, and I cordially invite you to join me in this spiritual self-examination.

A famous writer and Catholic priest has said, "In a world so torn apart by rivalry, anger and hatred, we [Christians] have the privileged vocation to be living signs of a love that can bridge all divisions and heal all wounds."[1] Make no mistake, this is a huge goal. But I think raising the bar for what will offend us should begin to make at least some difference in that good direction. As the psalmist writes in psalm 139, "Search me, O God, and know my heart! Try me . . . and see if there is any grievous way in me, and lead me in the way everlasting!" (Ps 139: 23–24).

1. Nouwen, *Life of the Beloved.*

"REMOVE THIS CUP FROM ME"

WE CASUALLY TAKE JESUS' prayer to mean "Let me avoid physical death," or "Let me avoid the pains of torture in this physical death." But in so understanding the prayer, we assume that physical death and physical pain are all that is meant by "taking upon himself the sins of the world." It is the typical assumption of a species that perceives nearly everything in terms of the physical.

But when Jesus speaks, he regularly places spiritual reality at a far higher level than physical reality. And when he heals in the physical realm, the healing clearly signifies a spiritual healing, just as his miraculous feedings indicate a spiritual nourishment.

Therefore, it is only reasonable to look for spiritual meaning in his prayer. And when we do, we begin to see that those three days in the tomb contained punishment for untold numbers of people over countless years. The human mind refuses to comprehend this magnitude of misery. We brush by it with the phrase, "He descended into hell," but the only way we can imagine the vast horror of it is to think of the slashing cords, the thorns in his scalp, the spikes in hands and feet, the suffocation, the exhaustion, and the shock that comes with massive blood loss.

That is a picture of the utmost reality of the undeserved punishment he endured, and we need that picture. But like all pictures it is only a sketchy précis of the real thing. Bible commentators often explain his forsaken cry from the cross by pointing out that "in that moment the weight of the world's sin fell upon the heart and being of Jesus; that was the moment when he who knew no sin, was made sin for us (2 Cor 5:21); and that the penalty which he bore for us was the inevitable separation from God which sin brings."

We can say, "Yes, this clearly is true, but I cannot imagine it." And that too is true, if by imagining it we mean experiencing it fully as Jesus did. But we can do our human best by remembering the times we have sinned grievously, and remembering what followed sin in our spiritual lives—the doubts that began to undermine our faith, the chill in our heart like a blade, the awful sense that the Father had given up on us, discarded us like a smashed piece of pottery, thrown us on a rubbish heap. Remembering those times, we can at least taste a tiny particle of the real pain Jesus felt after his physical death.

But of course there is always the remainder of Psalm 22, which ends on a note of triumph (not unlike Jesus' *Tetelesthai,* "It is accomplished"): The psalm Jesus quotes begins where he is at that moment, but it ends with a firm conviction that God has not abandoned us, that this forsaken feeling is both temporary and misleading, that unborn generations will serve him and will be freed by him. The promise is unshakeable, but so is the present sense of being lost, at least for the time being. Psalm 22 takes this human quagmire and follows it to our ultimate and welcoming home.

JESUS ON THE FAMILY

I think of the Christian organization called Focus on the Family every time I read in Scripture what the Lord said repeatedly about the value of family. Is it of greater value than obeying Jesus? I hope to show that making family our top priority is not the Christian way, though the value of family connections is in fact considerable among other worldly concerns. That's where it belongs, not in place of God's will.

In the gospel of Luke, Jesus clearly is aware, even at age twelve, that no less a being than God himself is his true father. In response to his mother's statement, "*Your father* and I have been searching for you in great anxiety," he takes her words "your father" and gives them a more accurate meaning. Jesus says, "Did you not know that I must be in *my Father's* house?" That house is the great Temple in Jerusalem, the Jewish house of God, not of Joseph, Jesus' adoptive father.

From early on then, Jesus knew his family was different, extremely dysfunctional. He knew Joseph was not his real father. That God was. The eminent New Testament scholar N.T. Wright confronts this difficult topic head-on with a list of Bible passages that indicate Jesus' position on the subject of family and its place. Here is the first one:

> "When his family heard the rumor, they went out to restrain him, for people were saying, 'He has gone out of his mind' . . . Then his mother and his brothers came; and standing outside they sent to him and called him. A crowd was sitting around him; and they said to him,

'Your mother and your brothers and sisters are outside, asking for you.' And he replied, 'Who are my mother and my brothers? And looking around him, he said, 'Here are my mother and my brothers. Whoever does the will of God is my brother and sister and mother.'" (Mark 3:21)

The biological brothers of Jesus are a curious group. First they are ashamed of one of his reputations, that He is insane, and want to take him home, presumably to hide him there. Then there is this next chilling passage, apparently some time later:

"After this . . . he didn't want to go about in Judea, because the Judeans wanted to kill him. The time came for the Jewish festival of Tabernacles, so Jesus' brothers approached him.

'Leave this place,' they said, 'and go to Judea. Then your disciples will see the works you're doing. Nobody who wants to become famous does things in secret. If you're doing these things, show yourself to the world. '" [And John adds:] "Even his brothers, you see, did not believe in him." (John 7: 1ff.)

So the Judeans wanted to kill Jesus, and immediately after saying so, John says Jesus' brothers urge him to go to Judea. They craftily advise him to show off what they probably dismissed as parlor tricks. "Turning water into wine? Does it all the time at home." And what is more, they see Jesus as motivated by a desire for fame rather than as a demonstration of God the Father's *agape* love. The brothers seem now to be running rampant, for by this time we no longer hear of Joseph. So without his paternal authority, the family is falling apart. In fact, when Jesus is on the cross, he has to designate John as head of the family, all of the others probably having left home to live with their wives and husbands.

We can if we like, say that this lack of order and wisdom is Jesus' reason for downplaying family ties in general, but that would be forgetting that John is not a biological member of the family. His only qualification, and it's a great one, is as a follower of Jesus, a member of the early church.

Now let's move on to the other passages so we can see more clearly the pattern of Jesus' sayings on this subject. "As he said this, a woman from the crowd lifted up her voice and said to him, 'Blessed is the womb that bore you, and the breasts that nursed you.' But he responded, 'Blessed, rather, are those who hear the word of God and keep it.'" (Luke 11: 27f.)

There it is again, on a different day and in a different context. Instead of *blessed be your mother*, Jesus prefers *blessed are the people who keep the word of God*. It's another way in which to place earthly families below spiritual ones. Let's hear the next one, in which one of Jesus' followers has possibly learned that the group is about to go on a journey.

"Another of his disciples said, 'Lord, permit me first to go and bury my father.' Jesus said to him, 'Follow me, and leave the dead to bury their dead.'" (Matt 8:21)

Does this sound outrageous? Well many scholars have pointed out that Jesus is here advocating behavior that his contemporaries, both Jewish and non-Jewish, would have regarded as scandalous: the obligation to provide a proper burial for your immediate family was so great that it overwhelmed all other considerations. But it is explained by the fact that Jesus held firmly to his concept that all Christians have an alternative family, the members of the Christian church. Besides, this is not by any means the only shocking thing Jesus said to his fellow Jews. Just think of his flexible attitude toward an extreme keeping of the Sabbath.

Next he quotes from the book of Micah on the subject, then adds to it himself. He repeats a passage from Micah when He says: "Do not think that I have come to bring peace on the earth. I have not come to bring peace, but a sword. For I have come to set a man against his father, and a daughter against her mother, and a daughter-in-law against her mother-in-law, and a man's enemies will be those of his own household. [And then Jesus adds the following.] The one who loves father or mother more than me is not worthy of me; and whoever does not take up his cross and follow me is not worthy of me." (Mt 10:34–9)

What are we to make of this today? Most emphatically *not* that we are to ignore our families. In all of the New Testament quotations that pertain to this topic, the choice is between Jesus (that is to say God's way) and the natural worldly way. When we say the Nicene

Creed repeatedly, it's a healthy reminder that we owe everything to God, including our having been born and being alive here today.

Furthermore, think of Jesus' positive attitude toward the family when he raises the Centurion's daughter to life, as He did Lazarus, not only for his own friendship with Lazarus, but also for the man's grieving sisters. And then there is the Samaritan woman's daughter whom he healed, and not least of these, his benevolent attitude toward the woman taken in adultery. This last probably because the woman was unwittingly tricked into committing adultery so as to form part of a trap for Jesus, but also because among the other taboos that Jesus cast aside was the inferior role of women.

It might strike us as significant in this study of Jesus on the family that the Catholic Church requires a newly elected pope to change his birth name for another more meaningful one, something also required of nuns and monks on accepting their vocation. I see this as a symbolic way of separating these people from their birth family when they turn their lives over to God, and to become part of a new family.

Obviously God created us in such a way that our biological family life (ideally) feeds us physically, protects us, and provides role models for us while we are maturing. But Jesus often points out that everything in our physical lives, even the best of things, is second-best. Nevertheless, when we have been away from our birth family for an extended time and then walk through the doorway into our family's home, and all faces look up at us from their card games or reading or cooking—look up at us with smiles, squeals and heys, get up and hug us, that unanimous welcome lifts our mood to one of joy—temporary joy, of course, but a little taste of heavenly joy nonetheless.

Probably another reason we find it easier to love our family above our love for God is because they are here with us in our natural life, visible, tangible, and audible, while we know of God primarily through his Son, Jesus. And we know Him only through his comments and actions as recorded in the Bible. But we know God's family, the Body of Christ, the church family, most especially at our local church.

Yet the question remains, Why would Jesus emphasize this point by repeating it so often? The Hebrew literature of the first two centuries is full of comments and statements on the value of family life. The sages tried to invest family life with an aura of holiness This artificial holiness allows us to see how first-century Judaism united an already precious Jewishness with an equally high value on the unadulterated family. There were to be no more Ruths marrying Jews.

Now we know why Hannah in 1 Samuel, could so easily sacrifice her first son to God. Both of them lived long before the first-century Jewish sages set up a policy that we can now see is not truly biblical. What both Jews and Christians need today is a focusing on God *before* we focus on the family.

There was a saying that made the rounds during the war in Vietnam. It went "My country, right or wrong." I'm not going to write about the war; I just want to examine the logic behind the saying. How do we know for certain what is right or wrong? Casting impulse aside as unreliable, we know it from some overarching system of ethics and morality, sometimes, if we're lucky, from our religion. But how can we call it our religion if we ignore its warning that something we're doing is wrong?

For there is a strong human tendency to worship things other than God. I'm using the word *worship* here to mean whatever we spend most of our time interacting with, considering and thinking about. If it's a raise at work, or our reputation, or approval by others, we are in spiritual trouble.

THE NATIVITY

ANYONE WHO PASSES THROUGH the night-time streets at Christmas is pretty sure to see lots of lights—often colorful lights, and maybe blinking lights, signaling a joyful season. Many people in our period of history like to festoon their homes with winter greenery (meaning life amid the appearance of a dying world), and with the color red (meaning exuberance and delight). That's our way of remembering and imagining the arrival on earth of the Christ child, and we are right to do so in the way we do.

But Luke paints a different picture of the Nativity. Not only is the birthplace a stable and the infant Christ's crib a feeding trough for animals, but we also have Simeon and Anna, two elderly prophets who were still alive at the time. Anna gives thanks to God that the Child has come to redeem Israel, clearly implying that Israel needed redeeming; and Simeon speaks of the infant Christ as being appointed by God for the opposition and fall of many in Israel, and that agony would pierce Mary's soul. Not a pretty promise at the birth of a king.

But this is Luke's picture of Jesus the Messiah's entry into our world. This drab plainness is in stark contrast with the promises given forty years earlier by the famous Roman poet Vergil, probably to some royal Roman child. The longish poem he wrote predicts the return of pure justice to the world, a new race of people brought about by heaven, a child who is to be born, evil to be eliminated, and the earth to be free from fear. The boy, he writes, will be divine, and in his kingdom the lion will lie down with the lamb. Snakes will die, and poisonous plants will wither. "Dear child," the poet writes, "great son of a great god, take up your honors."[1]

So gushes the great author on behalf of an earthly ruler. Is it any wonder that medieval Christians thought this poem was a prediction of the birth of Christ? It was, after all, as I said, written some forty years before the Bethlehem birth. Imagine then all of the hoopla, the lavish festivities, the banquets, the dancing, triumphal parades, the chanting—together with the thousands of lit torches and lamps—that would have followed such a human birth, with all its frailties. Now put that spectacle beside the birth of the *true* king of the world, Jesus. This of course is Luke's intent—to show in pictures what John said in the Prologue to his gospel, that Christ was in the world, the world that had been created through him, and the world did not receive him.

But we, presumably, have received him. That's why it is right for us to light up the landscape to celebrate his arrival. Every time we take into ourselves the communion wafer and the wine, our willing acceptance of Christ into our lives is refreshed, while at the same time we are reassured that we are accepted into his family, his body of believers and followers. Again, that is why it is proper for us to celebrate with millions of lights, and feasting, and the joyous giving of gifts, his arrival in our tattered world. Because we have accepted him as our true king, as Son of God, as the Second Person of the Trinity. We do not celebrate the birth of Dwight D. Eisenhower or of John F. Kennedy in the same way, and to my knowledge, no one proposes that we do.

But when we accept Christ as our king, what exactly are we accepting into our lives with him? It's all very well to speak of such abstractions as peace, justice, freedom and love, but those big concepts are always subject to differing human interpretations. Justice, for example, will mean to one person a legalistic and cruel judgment of a kind person, while to another it will mean protection of the same nice person from swindlers. Such terms are like rules for us to follow, and human beings can be extremely clever in looking

1. Virgil, *Georgics.*

as though they are obeying the rules while actually avoiding them. That's what some lawyers get paid for.

And that's why Paul says we are no longer under the Law. And that's why God did not send a memo with new rules for the New Covenant. He sent his Son instead, not only to *die* for our sins, but first of all to *live* among us, to live as a model for us to aim at, a completed human being in God's eyes and now in ours.

So how are we to learn from him how to be human? The only answer to that question that I can come up with is, "Watch him and learn from him." When he is merciful to the woman taken in adultery, but then tells her to stop sinning, we can learn from his action that to have *agape* love for a sinner does not mean that we should approve the sin of the beloved one. But we knew that already; it's just hard to remember it in a swiftly developing conversation, or in a highly emotional situation. And when Christ is ready to accept the rich young man as one of his followers until the young man refuses to stop idolizing his riches, we should learn that we can't expect everyone to fall to their knees every time we quote John 3:16. Even Jesus found some people to be adamant about their idolatry, and therefore about their unbelief.

Nevertheless, we should not ignore the passage in 1 Peter 2:22–23: "[Christ] . . . suffered for us, leaving you a pattern so that you could follow in his footsteps. He committed no sin. No deceit was found in his mouth; when he was abused, he did not return the abuse, and when he suffered he did not threaten, but gave himself up to the One who judges justly." Highly demanding? You bet. Because that's our goal, reachable only perhaps after a lifetime of intense effort. But unless we are unsatisfied with ourselves until God is finished with us, we will remain spiritually immature.

The risen Jesus tells his apostles to go out and make disciples from every nation. He says this once, and I'm positive he means it. But during his earthly life, according to the record of the gospels, he says "Follow me" at least twelve times, and always to different people. Now I personally take "Follow me" to mean "Walk the earth as I do from day to day," "Treat others as I do," and "Remember, as I do, that the Father loves his people and his creation; do not abuse or exploit them."

And why the emphasis on the life of Jesus apart from his death and resurrection? Because in order to bring others to accept Christ into their lives, we must first accept him sincerely into our own lives. Otherwise we are like the real estate salesman who urges people to buy land, sight unseen, that is mostly vertical, or is under water half of the time. Yes, he's probably feeding his family, but at the cost of being a hypocrite. (He knows that the land is unbuildable.) And Jesus had such strong negative feelings about hypocrites that he took the trouble to borrow the word from Greek, where it means "actor." It was a time when actors wore masks to indicate who they were pretending to be. So it's a dangerous thing for a Christian to only wear a Christian mask, to only pretend to be Christian, while continuing to live underneath it all as a pagan.

But guess what. There is hope even for the hypocrite. Even that can be forgiven, if only the person hiding behind the mask will come out and learn how to live as a Christian. The boy Jesus, Luke tells us, grew in wisdom. If even He had to learn the all-wise ways of the Father, so do we. And so do the people we convert.

And that takes us back to the Christ child in the manger, the King of the Earth, born under squalid and makeshift conditions. We too can teach the newcomer and feed the poor. It is the true Christian way.

That was typical of the very beginnings of Christianity and of the early church. If there was a manger at the Nativity, there was livestock, and you know what that smells like. There must have been, at best, a straw-filled stable for Mary's delivery of the boy-child. There is no sign of a midwife to facilitate the birth of this young mother's first child. And, most telling of all, if it had not been for the Magi, Herod probably never would have heard of his rival's birth. That's living out what Jesus means when he says the left hand (publicity) should not know what the right hand (love) is doing.

In modern terms, we would describe ideal Christian charitable love as second nature to the mature Christian—a second nature instilled in us gradually, drop by drop, as we cooperate with the Father, through his Son's teaching and example, and the Holy Spirit's inhabiting our bodies and our lives.

FAITHFUL ARTIST,
FAITHFUL ART

I ONCE MET A California Indian who made mobiles out of old forks and spoons and called it Indian art. I told him I hadn't known Indians had forks in the old days, but he said he didn't care about that. It was art, he made it and he was an Indian, so it was Indian art.

I have to admit I feel a little like that when I write a poem. You see, I'm what some people would call a Christian, so no matter what I write, it's Christian writing, faithful writing, faithful fiction. Or is it?

W. H. Auden once said religion has no place in poetry, or words to that effect, but he wrote a Christmas oratorio he called *For the Time Being*.[1] And three years earlier, in December 1938, he wrote "Musée des Beaux Arts," in which "the aged are reverently, passionately waiting/ For the miraculous birth," and "something amazing" happens—"a boy [falls] out of the sky."[2] It's Icarus in Breughel's painting, but the ancient myth of a boy falling from the heavens to his drowning death in the sea contracts neatly the "miraculous birth" of Christ and his death into a single action, an act of *kenosis* in the birth and sacrifice in the death, both sons under the direction of their respective fathers.

For us to deny that this poem, written while Auden was contemplating becoming a Christian, carries religious meaning is not only to deny the possibility of a poem's being subtle, it is also to

1. Auden, *For the Time Being*.
2. Auden, *For the Time Being*.

lose the magnificent Audenesque flat-toned statement that "there always must be children who did not specially want it to happen."[3] That is, there are always lots of people like Flannery O'Connor's Misfit who wishes Jesus had never risen from the dead.

And poor Gerard Hopkins, loving both poetry and God as he did, burned all his early poems when he became a Jesuit priest, feeling they were too much about the poet and not enough about God. But after he'd read Duns Scotus on the *haecceitas* or "thisness" of objects, he wrote "Wreck of the Deutschland," the forerunner of such gems as "God's Grandeur," "The Windhover" and "Thou Art Indeed Just, Lord, If I Contend." And George Herbert before him felt compelled to write about the reams of poetry dedicated to romantic love, and the sheer waste if at least some of that amorous energy were not dedicated to a love for God, clearly an apologia for his deft but powerful Christian poems.

And then of course there's Herbert's friend John Donne, who wrote both erotic poems like "The Flea" and Christian poems like the holy sonnets, perhaps at different periods of his life and perhaps not. And Milton, when thinking about his *magnum opus*, began his epic with an Arthurian theme, then abandoned it when he decided the Arthurian tales were fictional. Only then did he begin *Paradise Lost,* which tells us that he firmly believed in the divine events of his second epic, and yet had laid them aside for Camelot and the round table.

Do you see the pattern? Christianity has never been completely hospitable to poetry, in spite of the fact that the universal church has inherited the Hebrew Psalms as part of the canon of Scripture. Perhaps it's because the Psalms are written in a tradition of prosody that is foreign to most people, so they don't associate them with what they call poetry. Certainly the suspicious reception of poetry has been reinforced by the adherents of Modernist poetry, at least those who strive to be quirky, overly allusive, and just plain difficult to understand. But for whatever reason, Christian history has been colored by a distinct mistrust of poetry. Even hymns, inoffensive as most of them are, had a difficult time entering the tradition of

3. Auden, *For the Time Being.*

Christianity. We do have a body of Christian verse today dating from the earliest centuries of Christian history, most of it burdened with obvious (at least to us) truisms of the faith, some of it interesting, a smaller number powerfully moving and/or heartening.

And alongside this distrust of verse forms, there has been a long history of love/hate relationships with anything not easily labelled Christian. Tertullian, Jerome, and Alcuin of York all picked different targets ranging from Greek philosophy to classical Roman literature. But the Aristotelian thinking that Thomas Aquinas introduced to Western Christian theology is still in force today, and Neo-Platonism has made its valuable contribution as well, so Greek philosophy wasn't so diabolical as some people thought it was. And Jerome, who had warned the church about Roman authors, nevertheless loved them so much that he sifted the Bible for permission to let them in. What he found was a passage in Deuteronomy where God tells the Jews how to deal with one problem of warfare: what to do with pretty girls among the captives. To paraphrase, "If you wish to marry her, just see to it that she is shorn of all ties to her foreign culture, and make her a Jew. In this way you will provide sons for the Lord." Reading this allegorically, Jerome saw in it permission to embrace the pagan classics, providing one removes their immoral and idolatrous biases.

So the constantly recurring religious hunger for purity seems always able to find an acceptable way to bring the passerby into the wedding feast, as the parable has it. It's been said that there are two major types of thinking about the life of faith: the theology of hygiene and the theology of love. A little reflection on the gospels makes one doubt that Jesus would have had any hesitation in ranking love more highly than purity (while not dispensing altogether with some degree of purity). And yet the question remains, "How does the Christian poet go about adapting and adopting extra-Christian elements into poetry?"

And now I feel I must offer a reasonable answer to this question for Christian poets of any stripe. The answer I believe comes in two parts. First, if you haven't already found your own way, I suggest you follow Gilbert Highet's advice. In his magisterial survey of the classical tradition's influence on Western literature, Highet finds that the finest literature has come from writers who are neither the type of Christian who holds human nature in contempt, nor the sort of classicist who admires too fervently the ancient Greeks and Romans for their idealizing of human nature. Rather than those extremists, great literature seems to arrive through those who "have taken the best of paganism and transformed it [with] the highest of Christian thought."[4]

My first suggestion then is that poets allow themselves in their poems to admire some of human nature, but admire it only insofar as it might be either redeemed or allowed by what they see as the best of Christian thought. I leave it to them to find ways in which to do that. But I think they will find—as long as they truly see power in those non-Christian sources—that their power will come through in their writing. In this way they may very well help to overcome the universal church's suspicion of all poetry.

We saw Auden do this in "Musée des Beaux Arts," but to take it one important step farther I'll have to switch genres to C.S. Lewis's last novel, *Till We Have Faces*.[5] While a classical myth, Eros and Psyche, forms the backbone of the novel, with Christianity present only in hints, images and allegorical references, its beating heart is an even more valuable piece of advice. That one thing is my second point, one that is encapsulated in the novel's title: How can God meet us face to face "till we have faces"? And to have a face, one must say openly what has been lying at the center of us for most of our lives: the atheist's resentment of a supreme being merely for being supreme; the agnostic's keeping all evidence of the supernatural in a locked box buried in his cellar; the skeptic's pleasure in taking the role of the debunker, and the brittle delight of his cackle at what he calls gullibility.

Behind each of these masks lies an undeveloped face, which betokens an undeveloped identity. How can we, Orual finally asks, expect to be recognized by God if we are not yet honest human beings in our discourse with him? This rhetorical question is my second suggestion to Christian poets. Actually it is not just my

4. Highet, *Classical Tradition*.
5. Lewis, *Till We Have Faces*.

suggestion, it is Christ's attitude toward what he calls "hypocrites." Hypocrites, (actors) were and are people who pretend to be someone else, someone more significant, or at least more entertaining, someone who in ancient times wore a mask.

And so I cannot say strongly enough how important it is for us to achieve honesty—in our poetic voices, in our fictional characters, and in ourselves. I had read *Till We Have Faces* thirty years ago, but it had not occurred to me until more recently why it was so hard for me to pray. This time the novel helped me to see that I was avoiding all of the tough topics in my praying. I was like the occasional pastor who admits in his sermons sins like not spending enough time with his children, or the priest who confesses to not making his bed as soon as he rises in the morning. Yet each of them avoids the fact that one is keeping a secret bedmate on the side, and the other is filching money from donations. But once I had faced the being at the core of me, and the question it posed about my character, I began to show my truer face (and an altogether ugly one) to my God. It's a great relief to no longer keep a big secret. If you would be a healer through your art, it makes no sense for you to be a carrier of disease to your patients.

Napoleon once called England a nation of shopkeepers.[6] If an entire nation can be characterized by such a glib phrase, I propose as an American to label the United States a nation of salesmen. Call it advertising, or marketing, or public relations, or just being in business, we are beset by salesmen, and many of us are on our guard against them. Why? Because they are so often more interested by far in their image than they are in the quality of their products; because so many of them would like very much to sell us something they themselves would never own, something they have no respect for. We writers can perhaps do nothing about that sad fact, but we can avoid the pattern ourselves if we hope to showcase the best of our faith.

We could be sincere about our respect for people who resent a so-called "hidden" God, one who does not seem to answer their questions; if we were honest, we would admit to sometimes having

6. Smith, *Quotes of Napoleon.*

the same resentment. We could give more than lip service to the truism that changing one's world view is like living through a tsunami. (Actually for awhile it feels more like dying in a tsunami.) Let's not blithely dismiss the courage it takes to step out of a leaping boat onto waves like hills, expecting them to support our weight. One critic of Lewis's novel demonstrated what an astoundingly good job he did of this when he took Lewis to task, saying he liked very much the first part of the novel, but the second part felt like the same old apologist's snare.[7] What he revealed was that Lewis had accurately depicted the atheist's resentments, experiences and arguments in the first part. But what he ignored was that the second part was equally accurate about what happens once we speak honestly to ourselves and to God. The novel did not work for this one person, but it has worked for many others, in great part because the bulk of the novel respects the opposition and depicts it justly, giving it credit where credit is due.

And I think our poems, stories and novels are worthy of all the work we put into them even if they bring only one or two people to the point of asking the heavy questions: What are my resentments? What unexamined cultural assumptions of my time to I harbor? What are my real limitations and my strengths? What great fact about myself am I afraid to reveal? Does anybody really feel non-erotic love for someone else? If I were the creator of the person I dislike most, would I still wish that person were defamed or destroyed? What kinds of masks do I wear? Do I even have a real face?

7. McGrath, *C. S. Lewis—A Life.*

BIBLIOGRAPHY

Auden, W. H. *Collected Poems.* Edited by Edward Mendelson. New York: Random House. 1976.

———. *For the Time Being.* Princeton: Princeton University Press, 2013.

Barfield, Owen. *The Importance of Language.* Hoboken, NJ: Prentice-Hall, 1962.

———. "Poetic Diction and Legal Fiction." In *Essays Presented to Charles Williams.* Grand Rapids: Eerdmans, 1966.

Berryman, John, *Love and Fame.* New York: Farrar, Straus and Giroux, 1970.

Bond, Douglas. *The Poetic Wonder of Isaac Watts.* Orlando: Ligonier Ministries, 2013.

Brother Lawrence. *The Practice of the Presence of God.* Image, 1996.

Cecil, David. *The Oxford Book of Christian Verse.* London: Oxford University Press, 1940.

———. *Poets and Story-tellers.* London: Constable and Company, 1949.

Cicero. *On the Good Life.* Translated by Michael Grant. New York: Penguin, 2005.

Dobrée, Bonamy. *English Literature in the Early Eighteenth Century: 1700–1740.* London: Oxford University Press, 1959.

Ephraim the Syrian, St. *Hymns and Homilies by St. Ephraim the Syrian.* St. George Monastery. Lulu.com, 2020.

Gangel, Kenneth O. *Ministering to Today's Adults.* Eugene, OR: Wipf and Stock, 2006.

Gardner, Helen, ed. *The Faber Book of Religious Verse.* London: Faber & Faber, 1972.

Gardner, John. *On Moral Fiction.* New York: Open Road Media, 1995.

Gosson, Stephen. *The School of Abuse.* Whitefish, MT: Kessinger Publishing, 2010.

Herbert, George. *The Complete Poetry.* London: Penguin Classics, 2012.

———. *The Works of George Herbert.* Edited by F. E. Hutchinson. London: Oxford University Press, 1941.

Highet, Gilbert. *Classical Tradition: Greek and Roman Influences on Western Literature.* London: Oxford University Press, 1953.

Holmgren, Fredrick. "Barking Dogs Never Bite, Except Now and Then: Proverbs and Job." *Anglican Theological Review* 61 (1979) 341–53.

Lewis, C. S. *Mere Christianity.* New York: Simon and Schuster, 1952.

———. *Till We Have Faces.* Grand Rapids: Eerdmans, 1956.

———. *The World's Last Night and Other Essays.* New York and London: HarperOne, 2017.

Magnuson, Paul. *Studies in Romanticism.* Boston: Boston University, 1985.

McGrath, Alister. *C. S. Lewis—A Life: Eccentric Genius, Reluctant Prophet.* Tyndale, 2000.

Nouwen, Henri J. M. *Life of the Beloved: Spiritual Living in a Secular World.* Chestnut Ridge: Crossroad, 2002.

Rousseau, Jean-Jacque. *Les Reveries Du Promeneur Solitaire.* France: Livre de Poche, 1980.

Smith, Steve. *Quotes of Napoleon.* Independently published, 2020.

Virgil. *The Georgics.* New York: Penguin Classics, 2011.

Wood, James. *The Book of Common Prayer.* London: Penguin Classics, 2012.

Wordsworth, William. *The Borderers.* Tredition Classics, 2013.

Wright, N. T. *John for Everyone.* Louisville, Kentucky: Westminster John Knox, 2004.

———. *The New Testament and the People of God.* Minneapolis: Fortress, 1992.